CHARACTERS IN ACTION

A Guide to Playwriting

Marshall Cassady

UNIVERSITY
PRESS OF
AMERICA

LANHAM • NEW YORK • LONDON

Copyright © 1984 by

University Press of America,® Inc.

4720 Boston Way
Lanham, MD 20706

3 Henrietta Street
London WC2E 8LU England

British Cataloging in Publication Information Available

*Library of Congress Cataloging-in-
Publication Data*

Cassady, Marshall.
  Characters in Action.

  Bibliography: p.
  *1. Playwriting.   2. Drama-
Technique.   I. Title.*
PN1661.C36   1984   808.2   84-2277
ISBN 0-8191-3843-6 (alk. paper)
ISBN 0-8191-3844-4 (pbk.: alk. paper)

All University Press of America books are produced on acid-free
paper which exceeds the minimum standards set by the National
Historical Publication and Records Commission.

To Kim

ACKNOWLEDGEMENTS

I wish to express very special thanks to Jim Kitchen for all his help in the preparation of this book.

CONTENTS

INTRODUCTION

Characters in Action: A Guide to Playwriting is designed to get you started in gaining the experience that will enable you to write a produceable play.

It is my belief that characterization and action are the most important elements of most plays. Once you know your central character, you know how the person is likely to react. Then you can place him or her in various situations and with various other characters to show these reactions.

Throughout the years I've collected and developed the ideas included in this book both through my own writing and in various classes, seminars and workshops I've conducted for colleges, writing groups and a semi-professional theatre. What is contained here hopefully will help you develop your writing skill whether you are working in a class with others or writing on your own. The exercises are designed to lead you through initial idea to finished script.

There are few reasons for writing without a market or audience in mind. So the final chapter provides information on ways you can go about having your play produced or published.

CHAPTER I

THEATRE AND DRAMA DEFINED

Playwriting, like anything else, must be started with a first step. But the first step in constructing a play is different from the first step, for instance, in learning to play a musical instrument. Musicians learn first how their instruments work in order to produce a sound. Then they learn to produce the sound. The playwright, similarly, must know the workings of the theatre, but what is the first step in composing a play? Everyone already knows how to write. We've been doing it since we were in the first grade. Unlike the person who has to learn to make a buzzing noise with the lips to produce a sound on a trumpet, we already can "produce sounds." We've learned our basic scales and exercises.

A playwright cannot be told what should be the first step in writing a play because there are as many first steps as there are playwrights. Should one start with a character or with a bit of dialogue? Is the beginning a situation or a particular setting? These questions cannot be answered. It's up to the person who will be doing the writing.

It's been said that the only part of playwriting that can be taught is structure. But a number of modern plays have no recognizable structure. Can the playwright then be taught the art of composing dialogue? Again, some contemporary plays deemphasize dialogue. But if there is no dialogue and no structure, what's left? Characterization? There are many plays from Berthold Brecht's time to the present where characterization is not emphasized. The characters either are stereotyped or stripped of identity. They may even change from scene to scene, or shift roles from act to act.

Certain elements, of course, appear in a majority of plays, but if all we are left with is such an averaging, where does this leave those who want to learn playwriting?

Possibly, in a kind of limbo. But if you're interested enough and talented enough, you can emerge from that limbo. To do so you have to know theatre. Involvement in it is an essential for writing the successful play. It helps both to be acquainted with

1

current theatre and to know the major playwrights of each historical period. It's a good idea to have read Shakespeare and Sophocles, Ibsen and Maeterlinck. Seeing a variety of productions or even better, working on them, is also a help.

Theatre is an extremely broad area of learning, and no one can know more than a fraction of its history and practice. But to develop talent and skill as a playwright, you should attempt to learn all that you can. It's helpful to know what has worked already so you can try to judge what will continue to work. Part of this is being familiar with the various theories of drama from Sophocles to the present. It's helpful to know about such things as scenery construction and lighting practices, as well as heightening for dramatic effect and establishing three-dimensional characters. If you're not serious in your attempts at writing plays, you most certainly will fail.

DEFINITION OF THEATRE

The medium of theatre is difficult to define because it involves such a broad spectrum. A person's style of movement can be termed "theatrical" without the person's ever having appeared on a stage. The circus, the carnival and the ballet all can be considered theatre.

For purposes of playwriting, we can begin by defining theatre as the presentation of a play before a live audience. "Play" implies pre-planning and so would include well-plotted dramas by George Bernard Shaw as well as those by Jean-Claude van Italie, the latter of whom provided only an outline for The Serpent: A Ceremony, much the same as was done in the commedia dell'arte four hundred years ago.

Theatre can be defined further by distinguishing it from some of the other art forms. First, it is temporal. Once it has been presented, it's gone and can never be recreated in exactly the same way. Those working on one production have different interpretations of the script than do their counterparts in another production of the same play. One actor's appearance, movement and voice are different from those of any other actor. Stages differ in size. Properties and costumes differ from production to production. The show's run will differ from night to night. Actors continue to grow in their roles. They experiment; they attempt to find what will

2

work best. They are affected by the audience. If the house is responsive, they will be too. Theatre is unlike a painting that can be seen in the same state again and again.

Second, theatre is mimetic in imitating the experiences of humankind. It tries to have the audience identify or empathize with a character who is represented as real. The temporal and mimetic aspects combine to resemble life as it actually is lived.

Theatre also interprets. All the theatre artists add their own backgrounds, experiences and personalities. Through the way they view the work, they interpret events and actions and present differing viewpoints. No one person views life as any other person. The situations are colored; the recollections changed. All of these things become a part of the total production, which presents life in a particular way.

Theatre differs from other art forms in that it's a combination of forms which becomes something unique. It includes architecture in the settings; sculpture in plastic forms and in lighting; dance in the blocking and movement; painting in setting and makeup, and music in the flow of the language. It differs from many other art forms in that a number of artists work together to bring about a unity and a harmony in production.

DEFINITION OF DRAMA

Through limitation, we have a workable definition of theatre. Playwriting or drama may be a little more difficult to define. Theatre was defined in part by saying that it's a presentation which is pre-planned. The pre-planning is the drama, which can be a detailed script or a bare outline. Drama could be defined by saying that it is action and dialogue, portraying conflict in the form of a story and presented by actors on a stage for the entertainment and/or enlightenment of an audience. So by accepting this definition, we have a clearer idea of what drama is.

But still we may run into trouble since in some forms of drama there actually is no conflict. In 1963 the documentary play, In White America, had its initial production. In this play, as in many others written in the last few decades, there is no main character. When In White America was first produced, six people played

3

a variety of roles, some of them as oral interpreters rather than as actors. In White America expresses the viewpoint that blacks have been treated unfairly in America, and in part was written and produced to bring to the attention of the audience their plight from slave times to the present. The only real conflict the play produces is in the minds of the spectators.

Our definition of drama also included "dialogue" and "story." Dialogue sometimes isn't necessary, as evidenced in van Italie's Motel in which the two major characters destroy a motel room without the necessity of speaking to each other. And if story means a plot that builds to a turning point and climax, we outlaw many Absurdist plays, or those such as Waiting for Godot which have a circular structure. In this play two tramps wait for the appearance of someone named Godot, who never arrives. The two acts could be switched without seriously damaging the presentation.

As a matter of fact, to produce a play we don't even need a stage. Many plays are produced in nothing more than large rooms with a space in the center.

The definition also mentions "action." This is the most important ingredient and the only essential of all drama if we think of action as meaning "life." If people are alive, they are acting and reacting, even when they show no physical movement. Their brains are working and so are their involuntary nervous systems.

Taking all these foregoing elements into consideration, it seems that our definition of drama is incomplete in that it cannot be applied to all types. But it does fit one particular type, the story play, the kind that has a cause-to-effect relationship or a plot. Other plays throughout history and even in the present are in the minority.

In learning to write plays then this is a good place to start. In working with all art forms, the artist learns the rules before attempting to break them. So too a student of playwriting can probably best begin by closely examining the play with a plot.

Of prime consideration in the story play is the idea of conflict. In order to have conflict there must be opposition. The major character in the play, the protagonist, needs or wants something. He or she is opposed by the antagonist, which may take the form of a person, a group of people or a force. When the

4

protagonist's needs are established and then opposed, we have the basis for the action. We have the motivation which leads to the conflict. This struggle then continues throughout most of the play. If central characters are well-drawn, the audience should have no trouble in tracing their actions to the motivational base or the moment at which the conflict was introduced. Only in poorly-constructed plays does the central character appear to be unmotivated.

According to Aristotle in The Poetics, the earliest critical treatise we have on the theory of drama, a play should have a beginning, a middle and an end. This may seem to be obvious, but it does bear consideration. Aristotle meant first that a play should be complete in itself and contain everything necessary for us to understand it. It should exhibit a cause-to-effect relationship, with the dramatic question or problem introduced early in the play. It should provide a frame for the action or story line, established in such a manner that the characters and ideas can reveal themselves before the ending. There also should be a resolution, or a purification of the emotions.

Since the sixteenth century when Aristotle's writings on drama became widely known, he has exerted great influence on theorists and playwrights. But there is much disagreement with his views. There are those who feel that if a playwright follows Aristotle's definition the plays become too patterned or artificial. One argument is that since theatre is an imitation of life, there are no real beginnings or endings. Aristotle, however, stated that theatre should be an "imitation of an action," implying that first the central character meets an obstacle and then acts to overcome it. The action, though varied, continues until the tragic hero is defeated or the problem resolved.

Although Aristotle's views are not totally accepted, most people would agree that the audience does have to have some sense of ending, some feeling that the play has been completed. That is why we rarely see any true "slice of life" drama in contemporary theatre. Even if a play has no plot line that can be followed throughout, the audience has to feel either some sort of satisfaction or some sort of emotional release when the last-act curtain descends.

Not only do we need to feel this sense of

5

completion, but we want the drama we witness to mean something. Watching a family just "live" or go about their everyday tasks onstage would quickly become boring, so the drama has to be selective. Unimportant details are discarded. The action, the dialogue and even the characters are condensed. Time is compressed. Dramatists select the high points or the moments of direct conflict and forget extraneous material. Both in the past and in contemporary theatre there have been attempts at presenting life instead of art. But these experiments, such as "slice of life" plays and "happenings," though they continue to influence today's theatre, are in themselves no longer popular.

Drama like any other art form relies on certain techniques. Painters have colors, individualized brush strokes and composition. Yet they have to rely on certain established rules. They have to paint within a certain framework. A canvas, no matter what the dimensions, is still a form. The successful artist doesn't view this rectangle as restrictive; perhaps the unsuccessful artist does. Similarly, theatre has a structure, but within that structure exists freedom to experiment, to establish new techniques and to present new concepts.

Potential playwrights are more likely to be successful if they work within the security of a structure. Later, they may want to change what they do. But it's usually best to begin with the play that deals with a central character struggling against an obstacle. Such a play ends either with the central character's triumph or defeat.

The protagonist must never lose sight of his or her goal since much of the unity or focus in a play is the progress toward that goal. At the same time that a play is unified, it needs variety to hold audience interest. The complexity or variation occurs in the different situations the protagonist encounters, in the diversity of the other characters and in the different obstacles the central character meets. Variety is provided finally in the gradual revelation of the protagonist's character through the progression of events. Unity is needed for coherence; variety for interest and suspense.

THE ELEMENTS OF DRAMA

Aristotle also described the elements essential

for drama. They still are worth consideration in reference to contemporary theatre. From least to most important, they are **spectacle, melody, dialogue, thought, character** and **plot.**

Spectacle refers to the scenery and background. It enhances the play and gives the audience a variety of information. For instance, it can set the location and perhaps the historical period and season. It aids in creating the prevailing mood and often helps to establish character by giving clues to the economic and social levels of the major figures. Sometimes a setting establishes a character's profession and personality traits. It can demonstrate the tastes of the characters in the color, the architecture and the furnishings, and it provides clues about cultural background through the use of paintings or art objects. It can show the characters' interests and hobbies. Most important, it helps set the frame of reference for the play and establishes its levels of probability.

Melody refers to the rhythm and flow of the language. The emotional state of the characters and the emotional content of the situation should be reflected in the dialogue. The overall rhythm of a play depends upon its emotional content. Basically, the rhythm of a tragedy is slower than that of a comedy. Rhythm also is concerned with the matter of audience identification. Generally, the audience identifies more closely with the tragic hero than with the central figure of a comedy.

Dialogue refers to the speech of the characters. It must suit them and must be consistent with their backgrounds and personalities. It helps to establish the tone or prevailing mood of the play. To a large extent it establishes the changing tempos in the various scenes.

Thought or intellect is concerned with the playwrights' skill in constructing the plot or the vehicle for their ideas. The play should be both general and specific. That is, it should be the story of an individual but also should have a universal appeal. According to Aristotle, the play may have several themes or ideas, but only one should be dominant.

Character is the principal source for the development of the plot. Only through the speech and behavior of the characters is the plot advanced. The characters are the controlling force, and the play becomes unbelievable or artificial if fate controls them, rather than their being the prime movers of their own destinies. Things may happen to characters which are not of their own doing, but it's their reactions to these events which is the controlling factor in determining whether they succeed or fail in their struggles. Like intellect, character should be both typical and individual. A character must be an individual to appear believable but must not be so alien from others as to arouse no feelings of identification on the part of the audience. The character must be enough of an individual to maintain interest but also must help to illustrate a general truth.

Intellect and character in conjunction with other elements give the play a universal appeal. The play has to affect us personally through an appeal to our emotions. It provides situations, characters and events with which we can identify and through which we can learn.

Plot, the most important element of a play according to Aristotle, is the framework of the action in which the story line is developed. It shows the progression of events and enables the playwright to reveal character and ideas.

All the elements work together to accomplish the playwright's main purpose, whether it is entertainment, the statement of a theme, or the presentation of a feeling, a mood or a general impression.

CHAPTER II

PLAYWRIGHTS AND AUDIENCES

Chapter I has acquainted you with some of the hurdles in attempting to write a script. Maybe you already have an idea that can provide the basis for a play---an event, a bit of dialogue or a person you have observed. But before you become too involved in the writing there are two things you must decide. Why do you want to write a play? What audience do you want to reach?

It's rare to be struck with an inspiration that tells you what, why and for whom to write. Ideas usually come slowly and continue to grow. But before you develop your ideas into a script you probably should consider your reasons for writing. Possibly, it's for a better understanding of the composition and structure of drama. Or maybe you are a creative person who has a strong need to express yourself, and you feel that playwriting is the best form for you. There are any number of reasons that often overlap. Closely tied in to the reason for writing is the audience you want to reach.

CHOOSING YOUR AUDIENCE

Except possibly as a learning experience, there's no conceivable reason for writing a play without an audience in mind. Even if your only purpose is to prove to yourself that you can complete a play, you haven't really proved much if nobody ever sees what you write. A play is not complete without an audience.

In choosing an audience you want to reach, you can begin with general questions to ask yourself about the writing. This can help solidify your thinking about a subject as well. The first question could easily be: What sort of play do I like? Think of your own idea in terms of whether you would like to see a play on the same subject matter or with the same theme if it were written by someone else. If the answer is yes, go ahead with it. If it's no, you'd better do some more thinking. Even if the subject appeals to you, would it interest others? Why?

If you feel you have something important to say, how can you best insure that an audience will want to sit for two hours while you attempt to bring it to

9

them? Nobody's assured of success as a playwright, but by having a purpose in mind and by knowing the audience for whom you are writing, you have a much better chance of a successful production than the person who writes a play with no goal in mind for its being presented.

Neil Simon has often been criticized for the type of play he writes. His critics state that his plays say very little and that in ten or twenty years they'll be forgotten. Of course, people have been saying that ever since he first appeared on Broadway. And in terms of popularity he is the most successful contemporary playwright we have. This proves he's defined his reason for writing, and he knows his audience. His plays are primarily for enjoyment and entertainment and do not have deep philosophical or psychological themes. But why should they? He's reaching possibly the largest audience of any current playwright. He's not writing for the same audience as an Arthur Miller or a Mark Medoff. Nor will he reach the same audience as a Duerrenmatt or a Pinter. But his writing certainly fulfills a need for entertainment.

Although the divisions are not clear-cut and there's much overlapping among types of audience, people attend the theatre for three reasons: first, for entertainment or enjoyment; second, to gain insight into their own lives, and third, to learn. It's the escapists who want to be entertained. They want to get away from everyday monotony and problems. The kinds of things that appeal to them are comedies, thrillers and musicals. Then there are audiences who want to be taught. They may be seeking a way of life for themselves or they may want only to learn how others live. This second type is more likely to attend plays dealing with serious subject matter. Finally, there are those who view theatre only as an art form and who watch a play much as they would view a piece of sculpture. Most likely, revivals of older plays and experiments in theatrical form will appeal to this kind of spectator.

Each audience member may attend a play for a combination of reasons. And each may attend a wide variety of theatres: professional, community and educational, all of which can be sub-classified. There is educational theatre in which elementary and high school students participate, as well as educational theatre for college and graduate students. Many community theatres are completely nonprofessional, although quite often their productions are done as well as those of some professional groups. Then there are others in which the director, the designers and even some of the actors are paid but most of the company isn't. There is a wide range of professional theatre from those that present children's shows to summer stock companies to regional theatres using the star system. Broadway theatre is much different from off-Broadway and off-off-Broadway. The former stays with more traditional drama, while the latter is open to broad experimentation.

Each of these theatres exists for different reasons, and the playwright who hopes to be produced should know about these reasons. Basically, professional theatre exists to make money for the producers. Although some commercial theatres encourage writing by newcomers, they are in the minority. Community theatres exist mainly to give pleasure to as many people as possible. Therefore, each will produce plays that the members believe will be enjoyed. Often this is an excellent starting place for the new playwright. Many community theatres actively seek plays by new writers and even offer prizes for the best submissions during any season. If you do choose to write for a community theatre, you have a better chance of having your script accepted if you know the area and the type of people who attend plays there. A community theatre is more willing to take a chance on an inexperienced writer than is a Broadway theatre since there's not nearly so much to be lost if the play isn't well-received. The producing group in a community can have several financial failures and still survive; the producers of Broadway shows cannot.

College and university theatres also offer a better chance of production to the beginning playwright than does professional theatre. Educational theatre for the most part exists as a training ground. It can serve this function for the writer as well as for directors, designers, actors, technicians and audiences. Even if you cannot have your work produced as one of the school's major offerings, you often have the opportunity for workshop productions. Most schools have experimental theatres in which you are free to do as you choose with little restriction. Of course, you should be acquainted with the type of school, if not the specific school, for which you are writing. Some productions that might be acceptable at a large state university, for instance, would be rejected at a small, church-related college.

11

The type of play that can be done by an academic, a professional or a community theatre in one area may not be acceptable somewhere else. What draws an audience in New York City may leave a lot of empty seats in Indianapolis, Indiana. The moral outlook or general attitudes differ from area to area. A large city also has more of a potential audience of a particular type from which to draw than does a small community.

If you are from New Jersey or Maine, it would be presumptuous to attempt to write a play for a midwestern audience. On the other hand, if you are from the Midwest, you had better be familiar with what is currently playing on Broadway before you sit down to write a winner of the Drama Critics Circle Award.

Suppose you've investigated various theatres for which you want to write and have thought through your ideas. Now how do you interest the audience in what you have to say? How do you handle the subject matter? Well, that still somewhat depends on your purpose. Often, playwrights attempt to reinforce a common belief as Thornton Wilder did in Our Town. The play expresses very strongly that we should learn to pay attention to each other and make the most of our lives and our relationships. There is certainly nothing new in this idea, but Wilder states it poignantly and well, as evidenced by the continuing popularity of the play.

You've probably had the experience of seeing a play like Our Town which you felt stated ideas that were apparent to everyone. And since this was so, maybe you felt you could have written a play as well as the author did. Still you enjoyed the production. This is a common experience, and the playwright's ability to create this feeling is exactly what makes the piece of writing good. This is one reason Lorraine Hansberry's A Raisin in the Sun is a powerful play. The character, Walter Younger, a black man, finally realizes that true success in life can never come through compromising yourself and your personal dignity. All his life he's defined success as being synonomous with money. Then he's forced to choose between accepting a large amount of cash not to move into a white neighborhood or refusing it and retaining his self-respect. Walter, of course, makes the only decision he can. He and his family will move to the new house.

12

Although the theme of a play such as this states something apparent, maybe the author has explored the situation a little further or probed more deeply than others. At any rate, he or she has started the audience thinking.

On the other hand, a writer may deal with something relatively alien to the experience of the audience. Then maybe the goal is one of enlightenment. Historical plays often fall into this category, though many that do have other themes as well. For example, Peter Shaffer's The Royal Hunt of the Sun is set in the framework of Pizarro's conquest of the Incas in Peru. But it's also centered around a theme of lost faith. The play, Death of a Miner, is alien to most people in its story about coal miners in West Virginia, but, of course, it's concern with human rights isn't. And speaking of alien situations, science fiction plays also deal with strange settings and events. But whether they are concerned with alien situations, characters or social problems, all are dependent for success upon their ability to depict elements with which the audience can identify. The setting and situations and even many of the characters may be alien, but the play must deal with human emotions and problems even if the central characters are Martians or Venusians. Otherwise, the play can have little meaning for an audience. The viewer usually identifies with the central character, the protagonist. This identification is one of the goals of the majority of plays that have survived throughout history.

In contrast, Berthold Brecht is highly regarded for his Epic Theatre or Theatre of Alienation in which the ideas and situations are more important than the characters. When Brecht rehearsed his plays, he sometimes went so far as to have the actors add, "he said," or "she said," after each line. Thus, he felt, the performers would remain emotionally detached from the roles. He often allowed characters to appear for limited times only, thus helping to prevent audience involvement. Brecht emphasized social or political problems more than characterization, yet managed to express strong sympathy for the human condition. Even in Absurdist drama the human condition rather than the individual characters is important, since the characters often exhibit traits of automatism and speak with illogical or disjointed dialogue.

Another successful writer of the modern era was

George Bernard Shaw, to whom ideas often were more important than characters. Not many writers, however, can be successful with the technique of using long conversation on philosophy and religion as found, for instance, in the "Don Juan in Hell" scene from Man and Superman.

All these forms of writing were aimed at a specific type of audience, which accounts for their success. Any presentation, whether it's a speech, an interpretive reading or a short story, has to be presented with a certain audience in mind, even if the author has not consciously taken time to analyze the writing. The age, educational background, political leanings, social and economic circumstances, general views of life and geographic locations all have to be given consideration.

REACHING YOUR AUDIENCE

Maybe you have a theme, a character or situations in mind for your play. Almost any theme, if it's universal, can be presented. The manner in which it is presented, that is, the characters, the setting, the dialogue and the situations, are the determining factors in holding the audience's attention. Godspell, through its characters, situations and music, obviously appealed to a younger audience than did Evita, even though both had successful runs in New York. The former takes place on a playground and has a group of young people who enact Christ's parables and episodes from His life, as taken from the book of Matthew. Evita is a biographical opera about the life of Eva Peron, who rose to power in the 1940s in Argentina.

Another important aspect in planning a play is to consider its probability. Is Karel Capek's R.U.R. really believable? Will robots take over the earth someday? Are there really ghosts and witches as appear in Hamlet and Macbeth?

These plays deal with universals, but more than that the playwrights have set forth a certain frame of reference in each. The unusual or unbelievable elements from everyday life are believable within this framework. The playwrights have created a world in which these elements can exist.

According to Coleridge, theatre involves "the willing suspension of disbelief." However, Arthur Miller in writing Death of a Salesman probably never

considered having a robot bail Willy out of his
financial troubles. A certain framework was
established and an audience would be unwilling to
suspend its disbelief beyond that framework. Miller
built a framework that was close to the everyday
situation many Americans might encounter. He did
present expository material through the technique of
flashbacks which the audience was willing to accept
even though they had to imagine they were privileged to
witness the workings of Willy Loman's mind. Capek
depicted a society in which robots did exist. The two
playwrights presented frameworks that were believable.
Once they were established, the audience was willing to
suspend its disbelief so that the inclusion of unusual
or bizarre events didn't shock them. It's only when a
particular framework exists and then the author
deviates from it that the play becomes unbelievable.

For example, in a science fiction novel published
a few years ago, interplanetary travel was part of the
framework. The story dealt with a young man fleeing
execution. He could jump instantaneously from planet
to planet. Because this was established at the
beginning, the story was believable until the last few
pages. Then the protagonist escaped from his pursuer
by discovering a passage into a parallel universe. The
story ended with the central character's returning to a
slightly different home than the one he had left. The
universe he was now in was a similar though different
one. The story was ineffective in introducing the
escape to another universe since the existence of such
a place or the possibility of its existence hadn't
previously been mentioned. Thus the reader had no
preparation for the ending. Although disbelief about
space travel could be suspended, it wasn't logical to
introduce the new element of a parallel universe so
near the end of the story.

In other words, a story or play has to progress
logically with the characters attempting to solve their
own problems. Except if it's a spoof, it's unlikely
for any drama in which coincidence plays a major part
to attract a large audience. The central character
either triumphs or falls to defeat on his or her own
merits. Audiences are no longer willing to accept the
intervention of fate on behalf of the protagonist.
Such a plot is disappointing and members of the
audience are likely to feel cheated. Early events
should sow the seeds for the turning point or climax.
The detective attempts to discover who committed the
murder. As a member of the audience, you know it is

someone who has been introduced early on in the action. Any characters who play important roles in the outcome must be introduced early, either through actual appearance or through reference. It would be illogical if they were not.

In real life it's different. Police looking for a murderer may have no idea of the motive for the crime nor of the type of person they are seeking. Yet, crimes are solved. A suspect is arrested and subsequently tried and convicted. Perhaps the murdered person was robbed, and the murderer had no previous connection with the victim. In real life this situation would be believed. It wouldn't be in a play. What this shows is that one has to adhere to certain theatrical conventions in order to become a successful playwright.

THEATRICAL CONVENTIONS

A theatrical convention is a device used by the playwright, the designers or the director to improve or expedite the production. There are many theatrical conventions, some of them no longer acceptable. These include the soliloquy and the aside, used with much success in earlier years to compress or to reveal character and feelings. A comparable convention still in use is the monologue, in which the character talks directly to the audience as does the Stage Manager in Our Town. Flashbacks also may be compared with soliloquies. They both explain and they both can show the feelings of the character.

The entire idea of setting is a convention. An audience knows that the living room that appears on the stage isn't a living room at all but is made up of a series of flats. And rooms in houses are not arranged as those on stage. In a real house furniture is placed closer together to conserve space and the living room is much smaller than the one onstage. People on the street don't usually wear so much makeup as the characters in a play. Yet, audiences are willing to accept these make-believe devices.

There are various conventions used in writing a script. For instance, events progress faster on the stage than they do in real life. People cannot usually express their thoughts as explicitly or as concisely as do the characters in a play. Time is compressed and events heightened. There is selectivity of detail. An audience will accept all these things. Yet they are unwilling to accept coincidence, although it does sometimes enter real-life situations. They won't accept poorly drawn central characters they cannot get to know, even when they have lived beside the same neighbors for twenty years and barely know their names. Theatre is full of conventions that change from period to period. The playwright needs to be acquainted with how they can be made to work.

STYLES OF PRESENTATION

In order to write an effective script it helps to be aware of the various styles in which a production can be done. There are many styles of presentation and yet when the framework of each is established, they become reality for the audience. Overall, style may be broken into two categories, although the separation is arbitrary and no style is entirely pure. The representational style is one in which the action on the stage is presented as being true to life. The playwright is saying that what appears onstage can be seen outside the theatre. But by the very fact of presenting a patterned play on a stage, the purpose of duplicating life is defeated. It could be said that the representational style is a closer approximation of life than is presentational theatre. There have been many attempts to represent life in its entirety on stage, from having an actor turn his back to the audience at will to transporting peeled off wallpaper to the set of a production. Yet despite all attempts at representing life, the actors spoke memorized dialogue, the director planned the exits and crosses and the play took place in a theatre specifically set up for a production. Audiences viewing a production of Tobacco Road know that the action takes place on a stage that is covered with a few inches of sawdust or dirt that only represents poor Southern land and is not the land itself. But no matter what the style, the audience is willing to accept it if it's established at the beginning of the play.

The presentational style is audience-centered rather than stage-centered. The actors admit the existence of the spectators and even talk directly to them. Many readers' theatre productions fall into this category as do plays in which the characters deliver monologues directly to an audience. Often a bare stage is used or elements of setting suggest rather than portray. What scenery there is usually is nonrealistic. Ancient Greek drama was largely presentational since little scenery was used and the chorus, in particular, often spoke directly to the audience. The actors wore masks and high-soled boots, and the movements, it is believed, were expansive. Drama in the public theatres in also had many elements of the presentational style since, apparently, there was little or no scenery.

No style is pure. For example, is presentational in that it does not use scenery, and from time to time a character speaks directly to the audience. It also is representational in that the actors sometimes move into specific scenes in which they don't recognize the presence of an audience. Then there are scenes, such as the one at the soda fountain, which are a mixture of the two styles. The Stage Manager assumes another role while George and Emily keep the same roles they have throughout the play. Musical comedy is highly presentational in the use of singing and dancing but often is representational in the dialogue.

Even in a play that would be classified as representational, the actors usually play to the audience. Unless there's a reason or a specific effect desired, they usually don't turn their backs on the spectators. Furniture isn't placed across the front of the proscenium opening. All the other styles of theatre, such as naturalism, expressionism and symbolism are offshoots of these two styles and lean more strongly to one or the other.

Besides considering style, it helps to be aware of differences in theatre structure. It would be difficult or at least ineffective, to present with all its spectacle in a theatre that would lend itself to a production of the much more subdued . The latter demands intimacy and a smaller stage and theatre, whereas the former involves much more physical movement.

As a playwright you need to consider the practical aspects of , including such things as how easily a certain type of setting can be constructed, how long it takes for set and costume changes and the problems of shifting and storage. Modern audiences don't want to sit and wait for extensive set changes. You have a better chance of writing a produceable script if you know the theatre's limitations. You need to consider how much actual change is needed and how it can be accomplished.

You need to keep up with current trends in theatre and know about the structure and genre of plays. You need to analyze the audience. At least as important as anything else is working with as many productions as possible to learn all you can about the practical aspects of presenting a play. In any theatre you have the chance to volunteer to work on lighting or set construction or costuming---whatever is needed. Then finally you can be ready to begin the actual writing of a script.

But what do you do first? Where do you actually begin? Some playwrights state that they begin with a theme or an idea they want to express. Others begin with a character who may be based on someone they know or have observed. Still others start with a bit of dialogue which may have come from an actual conversation. Sometimes a setting or a situation can suggest a starting point. It's up to the individual playwright to sort out ideas and impressions before attempting to put them down on paper. It's rare for someone to sit down to write a play without having a combination of the foregoing ideas. One thing is certain: the more you write the more ideas you'll get for writing. It's as if the mind becomes geared to sorting out ideas for plays or stories. Many writers have expressed regret that they will never have the time needed to write everything they want to write.

One device that many writers use is to sit down at a typewriter and write the first word that comes to mind. Mechanically, they start adding words until an idea develops. Some start writing nursery rhymes or adages which they hope will start them thinking. Others begin by putting down the word, "The," followed by any noun and then any verb. Some use word association to get ideas.

You can also use the latter technique to develop characters just by arbitrarily stating things about him or her. For example, Sex: male. Age: forty-five. Marital status: divorced. Number of children: three. Occupation: construction worker. Address: Brooklyn. The process is carried on until an individualized character is created. This is an artificial way to begin writing, of course, but if you have no ideas that you like, it can work. On the other hand, many characters are based on something from the writer's own experience.

A character in a play may not necessarily be based

on one individual but may be a combination of real-life people the author has known. The playwright chooses, adds and combines the traits to be emphasized. No character from life can be transferred directly to the pages of a script. First, the author will view a certain person in a different light than will anyone else, and, second, characters in a play will develop and grow individually and of themselves if the playwright allows it.

SUMMARY

To be successful as a playwright you should learn as much about theatre as possible. You should know about historical periods, the styles of writing and production, the structure of a play and the type of theatre and audience for which you are writing. You need to have a purpose in mind. Individual authors then may use any number of approaches, but they need to establish a frame of reference in which all the actions are logical. Then the protagonist has to determine the outcome of the play.

The playwright should be aware of theatrical conventions and decide upon the overall style in which to write.

EXERCISES

1. Analyze a particular theatre and evaluate the types of plays that could be presented there.

2. Choose a nonrealistic play and evaluate how successful the author has been in establishing and maintaining a logical framework.

3. Make a list of theatrical conventions used now and in the past and discuss their effectiveness.

4. Read a modern play and determine whether it is largely representational or presentational. What elements of each style does it contain?

5. Analyze and evaluate one of the newer trends or styles of playwriting.

6. Develop a character through the question and answer (word association) method.

7.   Develop a setting or circumstances for a play through the word association method.

8.   Read a successful modern play and attempt to determine the reasons for its success. What particular type of audience does it appeal to? In what way?

9.   Investigate a theatre that is willing to produce a new playwright. How does the playwright submit a script?

10. Read a pre-twentieth century play and a contemporary play. Evaluate and compare their universal appeals and their immediacy.

CHAPTER III

CHARACTERIZATION

Character is one of the most important aspects of a play. Even if a dramatist doesn't start with a character, a principal figure usually is necessary as the primary means of developing the plot and of stating the theme. The type of character chosen often determines the environment. Even the situation is to a large extent prescribed by the characters since any person placed in a specific set of circumstances will react to those circumstances in a different way than will any other person.

Character is that element of a play with which the audience most closely identifies. There are exceptions. In some plays character is deemphasized and audiences empathize with the plight of an entire group of people or with a social condition. But in most plays it is the character as an individual for whom the audience feels empathy or sympathy.

Quite often ideas for a play come from the development of a particular figure. Suppose the character who comes to mind is one who's completely self-centered. The author will think of a situation in which to place this person so the extent of the selfishness can be revealed. Next the writer chooses other characters with whom the central figure can react. The situations suggest the conflict, from which the remaining elements of the play can be developed.

KNOWING YOUR CHARACTERS

None of us knows how we will react to a new situation. We can only guess. The same is true of the characters. As the writing progresses, they often tend to take over the actions. Still, you should know them well enough to know how they are likely to react. What will cause them to flare up or back down? If they are threatened, will they retreat or will they lash out? Are they easily defeated, or will they accept no defeat?

The more planning that is done before the writing begins, the better. It helps to know much more about a character than ever will be revealed in the play. Characterization can be compared to a building that has

many sub-levels. Only a small part of the total
building is visible, just as in life only a small part
of a person's psychological makeup is revealed to
others. Similarly, a large portion of the character is
buried below the surface, but there is a depth from
which to draw. Because of a character's background and
experiences, he or she will react believably, but
differently from another character in any situation.
To have the characters appear to an audience as
three-dimensional complete human beings, it helps to
know them as well as you know your closest friends or
relatives.

Once the characters are developed, they often take
the action into their own hands, sometimes even to the
extent of determining the direction of the total
script. So when you put the protagonist in a situation
with other characters, you need to give him or her free
rein. As a result, there usually is no need to force
dialogue upon the characters. To force them to go any
way other than the direction they themselves take may
come across as artificial. By allowing the characters
to speak for themselves, you may receive some
surprises. But when examining their psychological
basis and background, you'll discover that the speech
and actions were logical or predictable, even though
the subtleties of development may have been
unexpected.

Most successful plays focus on one character, even
though others may have as much dialogue or stage time.
Consider, for example, such diverse plays as Hamlet
with its tale of revenge and Peer Gynt, a fantasy.
Though the characters are completely different, one an
indecisive prince, the other a rogue, the play focuses
on one person. Even in Gerhardt Hauptmann's The
Weavers there is only one important character, although
it is a collective one.

There are exceptions as can be seen in The Bald
Soprano and The Changing Room. The former has
characters literally without identifiable personalities
of their own and none of whom is emphasized over the
others. The second play is concerned with a
semiprofessional rugby team where, although the
characters are individuals, none is most important.

The majority of plays, however, do have a central
character which may be developed in many ways. What
follows is an example of one way. In one of my own
plays the central character was named Rita. At

thirty-two, she still held onto unrealistic dreams of a life of glamour. The germ of the idea for the play came from a magazine story about a selfish parent. What evolved was a person who was unable to accept an adult role in life. She had always had dreams of bettering herself and of rising above her early environment. Because she saw glamour in a life in the theatre, she grasped the idea of becoming an actress. Her dream of adulation and financial success was totally unrealistic, based on nothing more than that she appeared in a high school play and received the praise of her drama coach and members of the audience.

Rita's father was a sporadic worker, usually too drunk to hold a job. Her mother, a chronic complainer, finally drove her husband into leaving home.

Rita has been married for nearly eighteen years. She and her husband started dating in the tenth grade. Rita was flattered by his attention, and from this involvement she became pregnant.

Rita feels that she missed out on much of the fun and excitement of being young, so aging becomes a serious problem for her. As the years pass, she fails to admit that the possibility of leading a glamorous existence is becoming more remote.

After the central character was worked out in more detail, I considered the characters with whom Rita could react to bring out the idea of her unrealistic goals. The most logical and obvious was her husband. Thus emerged the character of Howie, who also became a leading figure in the play. Establishment of these two characters suggested the children, Billy, with whom Rita was first pregnant, and Susie. Then I analyzed Howie and the two children in much the same way as I'd done with Rita.

After the four characters were developed, I let them speak to each other on paper without consciously trying to guide what they said or did. The major conflict was suggested by Rita's refusal to give up her dreams. When the play opens, Rita and Howie have just paid off all their debts. Now Rita wants to make up for lost time and recapture the fun she felt she missed out on.

Through the situations in which the principal characters found themselves, the other characters were evolved to complete the play. Four remaining

25

develop them as fully as the members of the family.

Several points can be inferred from the foregoing. First, the character of Rita was to dominate the action of the play, so her personality was developed fully before she was placed in a situation with others. To accomplish this goal, it became important for me to know her in detail---not only her past life but her desires and longings. She had to be explored and developed both emotionally and psychologically The characterization suggested the situation. Before getting too far along, I made a brief outline but kept in mind the idea that the characters should be allowed to develop the plot themselves. What evolved was somewhat different from the basic outline, yet appeared to be more appropriate to the characterization.

Writers probably would have difficulty developing anything that was in any way convincing if they didn't learn to know their characters beforehand. Such knowledge doesn't come in a flash but is a slow process, just as it is a slow process to learn to know someone who will later become a friend. Certainly, you form first impressions of other people, but these impressions often aren't lasting. You have to know people longer than a few minutes before you can begin to understand their personalities. You learn to know characters in a play by analyzing them in much the same way an actor may analyze a role.

One of the first things is to figure out the characters' physical attributes, including height, weight, eye color and any distinguishing features. Then you try to determine what makes them individuals, different from others of the same general type. What are their tastes in clothes? My character of Rita, for instance, was short and bouncy, with a false gaiety, assumed to convince herself she could have fun. She had brown, curly hair, cut short, and she wore tight-fitting dresses or sweaters and short skirts to make herself appear younger than she was. She could have been pretty except that her features were too sharp, too pasted on with an overuse of makeup. It is obvious that the physical appearance over which a character has some control, for instance, hair style, clothing and makeup, will follow a certain pattern because of the character's feelings and attitudes about life. You need to figure out the how and why of the character's psychological aspects. Of course, a director may see the character as physically different, because of the character's feelings and attitudes about life. You need to figure out the how and why of the character's psychological aspects. Of course, a director may see the character as physically different, and few actors will exactly fit your conception. But to visualize the character and make him or her real and clearcut, it helps to visualize the person as completely as possible.

You also need to know the characters' backgrounds. Where did they grow up? Were their families poor or wealthy? How did the economic situation affect their outlook? How much schooling have they had? What are their interests and hobbies? What kind of work do they do? Are they happy with their jobs or would they rather be doing something else? If so, why?

What kind of speech patterns do they have? Is it affected by the location where they grew up, by their schooling or by their present environment? How does their speech reflect their personalities? What is their vocal quality? How are other people likely to view them? Would others like them? Why, or why not? What were the biggest influences in their lives so far? What in their backgrounds has caused the biggest changes in their outlook? Are they basically optimistic or pessimistic, basically introverted or extroverted?

What beliefs and attitudes do they hold? What brought about these beliefs and attitudes? Was their early background strict, or did their parents give them a lot of freedom? Did the parents care about them? What were their parents' relationship with each other? How did parental attitudes, habits, living conditions and environment affect them? Do they like other people?

What are their dominant traits? Are they moral persons? What do they hope to accomplish in life? What are their main goals? What are their drives? How do they define success? Are they envious of others? Are they bitter toward life? How are they likely to act in any given situation? All of these questions will not be answered directly in the script, but they will allow you to know and project your character as a three-dimensional individual, not as a cardboard caricature. Much of this information can be introduced into the exposition of the play so that the audience can better understand the characters' motives and the reason for behaving in a particular way.

All of the major or leading characters can be analyzed, using the questions mentioned above and any other questions you think are important. Then you need to examine the relationships among the characters. What do they think and feel about each other? How do they react with each other?

To make the characters credible it helps to understand the motivating force behind each and to be able to empathize with their situations. An important idea to keep in mind when analyzing your characters is that unless you are writing a play in which characterization isn't an important element, it's probably best to make all your leading characters complete human beings whose actions can be understood, although not necessarily condoned. Understanding your characters goes a long way in making an audience respond to them.

Of course, creating characters is a subjective process. The things you write are your perceptions of the world. They show how you feel and what you believe. Often our characters are different parts of ourselves. It would be nearly impossible to find a character who is completely alien. Each human being has the basis or potential for developing nearly every personality trait. Others may have talents in areas we do not, or abilities to do things we cannot do. Still, we relate to others. But if we could go back and arrange a different set of circumstances for our early lives, we probably would be totally different people. Thus, there are bits of everyone's character traits in us, and bits of our traits in everyone else. We aren't all murderers or potential murderers, but in certain circumstances most of us could be. But more than that, even murderers have some positive traits. They have some characteristics with which we can sympathize or identify. It's up to the playwright to find these traits in their characters and then to portray them. Otherwise, the characters may appear as all good or as all evil, and they won't be believable. They wouldn't interest us either because if they were certain of their actions in every set of circumstances, as is likely if they are either completely good or bad, there would be little conflict in their lives. And conflict is important in holding our attention in most plays.

DETERMINING THE DOMINANT TRAITS

After developing your main characters, you need to decide what traits of those characters you want the audience to see, which facets of their personalities are important for understanding the play. Even though you know your central characters fully, the audience doesn't or can't. There just isn't time. And so the major characters have to appear simpler than people in real life so the audience can easily grasp what they are like. This can be done through exaggeration and pointing up important facets of their personalities. In certain ways a novelist has an advantage over a dramatist. The former can write long paragraphs about characters' personalities and backgrounds, their motives and actions. The novelist can explain in detail why characters are as they are. The expository material in a play can be brought about only through appearance or dialogue. Novelists can write as many pages of text as they wish. Dramatists are limited to approximately two hours of playing time. With this constraint they can concentrate on only a limited number of personality traits. If you try to show too much about a character in a two-hour period, the result will either be confusing or will not be fully explored. The character may come across as vague rather than as being well-developed.

It often is a good idea to think of your characters in terms of goals or drives. What does each want the most? What is the major goal that can realistically be explored and opposed in the time it takes for the three acts of the play to progress on the stage? There may be secondary goals, but if they become too important, again the audience may be confused. Of course, the play will deal mainly with the protagonist's struggles to reach a goal. But other characters also have needs and wants. If the antagonist is a person, his or her drives are directly opposite the protagonist's. Even within each scene, the characters have reasons for being there, and these reasons are their goals.

CHOOSING THE NUMBER OF CHARACTERS

Need should be the guide for inclusion of minor characters. Only those necessary to advance the play should be included. It's difficult enough to present a few traits of one character without introducing a host of unnecessary persons who have wants and needs of their own. Each extra character takes away from the time that can be spent with the major character. You have no doubt seen a play in which a minor character "stole the show." In a review of the play the drama critic may have attributed this to the acting of the person playing the role or to the weakness of the director in allowing it to happen. It very well could have been the playwright's fault. The writer could have allowed the minor character too much latitude. Perhaps the character was developed too fully and allowed to run away with the scene.

It's important to remember then that the major characters have to be fully developed, but the minor characters should not be. If they are, there is the danger the audience will identify too strongly with them; that when they appear for only a scene or two and don't come back again, the audience will be disappointed or will want to know more about them.

Often certain auxiliary characters are needed to further the action, but they should be considered only as dramatic devices. Suppose a character is a landlord. His function is to provide conflict for the main character who is behind in his rent payments and gives noisy parties. The landlord appears briefly to threaten eviction. There is little need for the audience to identify with him or even to understand the type of person he is. He's only a device and should remain as such. There's no need to analyze his whole personality. It can be assumed that his goal in the context of the play is to make a living, so he must have the monthly rent check. He also must keep the other tenants happy so they won't move. One way to keep them happy is to make sure that others don't intrude upon their privacy by making unnecessary noise. We don't need to know anything more about him than that, if his only function is to complicate matters for the protagonist by appearing in just one or two short scenes. Generally, the less characters appear, the less we need to know about them.

Because no character is entirely alien to us, each has common traits. So to a degree each then is a type. There's no need to develop those characters included merely to further the action, other than perhaps to give them a distinguishing trait or two. But in such a case as the landlord the audience doesn't need to know anything other than that he is a typical landlord. To individualize him too much would be to detract from the central characters.

30

All characters have to be stereotyped or typified to a certain extent for members of the audience to be able to identify with them. Such typification often means only that the character has to possess universal qualities. Since characterization cannot be fully revealed in the length of a three-act play, the spectator needs to be able to assume some things. If the audience members see someone who appears to be of a type with whom they can identify, they will have no trouble in assuming certain things about the person. You don't then have to express them openly. For example, the audience could safely assume that a typical mother and father would be concerned about their children. On the other hand, if the major characters don't have distinctive traits of their own, things that set them apart from others, the playwright hasn't made them believable. There has to be a balance between typification and individuality.

Another general rule to follow is that the characters in tragedies usually are developed more fully than those in comedies in that the audience most often identifies more closely with them than with the comic hero. It stands to reason that we might feel hesitant about laughing at someone whom we know well and with whom we identify. Of course, in some comedies we laugh <u>with</u> instead of at a character, who is able to see the humor in his or her own situation. Then, of course, we can identify with the person without having guilt feelings.

CHOOSING SCENES FOR THE CENTRAL CHARACTERS

Once you have drawn your characters, where does the actual writing of the script begin? As close to the climax as possible. To provide interest, to build suspense and to hold attention, all the scenes in a play should be important. Anything not essential to the plot only detracts. An exception is in intensely dramatic plays where the author feels a need to include some comic relief. This can contribute to the overall effect of the play by providing contrast and thus pointing up the serious content.

A reason for including certain scenes is to reveal character. There are several ways of doing this. One is through dialogue among other characters. But we cannot learn much about other people just by hearing about them. Others' views are colored by their own personalities. We have to meet a person to find out important or outstanding qualities. Physical

31

description also is unreliable. Unless people have a distinctive physical trait or wear clothing that makes them stand out, we are usually not able to describe them well enough for another person to pick them out of a group. Even if we see an individual for the first time and, for instance, that person happens to be asleep, we cannot know much about him or her. We must see people doing something or hear them talk.

So the second way to learn to know a character is to see the person acting and reacting. The best way of revealing or portraying characters is to present them in action. We learn about them by the way they meet crises or handle conflict. We discover the most, for instance, about Walter Younger in A Raisin in the Sun by seeing him in conflict with the neighborhood representative. This confrontation shows facets of his personality that were previously buried below the surface.

When characters are opposed in any way, we learn more about their emotional and psychological characteristics. We can tell a great deal about the characters by what they do when their goals or drives are opposed. Reactions to crisis or conflict may reveal things the people may not even know about themselves.

A play should include situations in which the goals of the character will be questioned or opposed, where drives will be thwarted. When the opposition becomes the strongest, the most important qualities of the character will be revealed. It can then be seen how far characters are willing to go to achieve an aim. Willy Loman will kill himself, for instance, rather than face the fact that he's not lived up to his definition of success.

It's when we see how far a person will go to realize a goal that the basic personality is best revealed. One of the main objectives in revealing character in this manner is to hold the attention of the audience, and the best way to hold that attention is to make the spectator want to know how the character will respond to a particular set of circumstances. We want to see what lengths Oedipus will go to in trying to end the plague in Thebes and why he persists even after he realizes the search for the murderer of Lais will end in his own destruction.

REVEALING CHARACTER

It's a common misconception that the central character of a drama has to undergo a massive change or a personality reversal. Such a change isn't logical. Personality has been determined by a human being's entire background, so it's not reasonable that one major crisis should cause him or her to reject all that has gone before and undergo complete psychological and emotional change.

Instead of any massive change or reversal, we have character revelation. A part of a character's personality that wasn't apparent previously is revealed. The revelation occurs gradually throughout the play. If the audience were to see the total character at the beginning of the first act, they probably would have little interest in the play's outcome. Any revelation must be logical in view of personality and background. Characters may change their minds or their courses of action or even their goals. But such changes are brought about by something already inherent in their personalities. The changes result only from seeds already growing and that maybe even the characters themselves failed to recognize. It's often been said that adversity best shows a person's true makeup. When faced with trouble, the strong often become weak and the weak become strong. A character in a play is no different.

Even if a character is defeated, even if the person commits suicide or is driven insane, the potential for that suicide or insanity must be there before the event actually occurs. For example, in Death of a Salesman, Willy Loman does commit suicide, but his death comes as no surprise.

DETERMINING THE PLAY'S OUTCOME

The climax of any good play must be a logical outcome not only of what has happened previously, but also of what is an inherent part of the major character's makeup. We know that the two main characters in Neil Simon's Barefoot in the Park will "live happily ever after" despite the fact of differences in opinion, style of living and background. We know this because of their love for each other, which is the most important emotion felt by either. A similar idea can be found in the comedy Mary, Mary by Jean Kerr. Mary's basic need is to be loved for what she is, without having to play the role of a sensible girl. Bob's need is to be loved and cared for, to be dependent upon someone. The conflict in the play deals with the two characters learning to accept things as they are. The conflict superficially seems to be between Mary and Bob. But it really is between the characters and themselves. In the end, instead of fighting against themselves, they learn to accept what is and to live with it. Since an audience often is aware of what the ending of a play will be, the real suspense is concerned with how this outcome will be achieved, how the characters will either win or lose.

When beginning to write a play, it's a good idea to try to decide what situations will best reveal the dominant traits of your characters. For example, if a man has an overwhelming drive to succeed at his job, he can be placed in a situation where this drive can be tested. Suppose he has a chance for a promotion, but two of his co-workers have the same chance. How does this affect him? How does he act with the co-workers, with his family and with his boss? Put him in situations with each of them and find out.

How does he react to his wife's accusations that he's spending too much time at the office to the detriment of his family? How does he react differently when the issue of overtime comes up again during a conversation with his boss? How does he treat his co-workers? Does he fight with his wife and kowtow to his boss, or does he feel guilty about spending so much time at work and thus try to make it up to his wife in other ways? Does his situation cause him to resent his boss? The type of character he is will answer these questions. We must see him in the situations to know the answers. We can learn much about characters by seeing how they react in one situation as opposed to another.

You can begin by placing your characters with others. Often one situation will then suggest another. For instance, the characters may discuss an upcoming event, which suggests a later scene you may want to include. Seeds for any important action have to be planted ahead of time by the playwright. Or else the audience feels cheated. The characters not only speak to themselves but also foresee situations in which they may later be placed.

But keep in mind that the characters should control the action. The plot cannot be imposed upon

34

them, or the action will become artificial. At the same time, the progression toward a climax must be both plausible and clear. The play shouldn't ramble. The character wants something, and the play is the story of his or her efforts to get whatever it is. If the author knows the characters well, the actions will be clear and the plot will be plausible. Every situation that is first included in the play may not be a part of the finished script. Some scenes may have to be cut and others trimmed to hold the audience's interest and to make certain that the play reaches as quickly as possible from the introduction to the conflict to the climax. The playwright has to be selective.

Another consideration in building character is choosing names. Obviously, the names should suit the characters. For example, "Jim" may suggest an honest, straightforward person, while "Algernon" seems to imply an affected, artsy type. The best advice for choosing a name is to consider all the connotations. The more common the name, the less connotations it will have and the more realistic or universal it will seem. During the eighteenth century in England such characters as Lady Wishful and Lady Sneerwell, through what they were called, told the audiences exactly what kind of people they were. The danger of such a practice is in making the characters seem to be merely caricatures.

SUMMARY

Character is one of the most important elements of plot since it is the primary means of stating a theme or of bringing a play to life. Because of its importance, you should be as inclusive as possible in knowing your leading characters. Character also is important in that it is the element that most often provides the interest and the sense of identification on the part of the audience. If an author starts by choosing one character, this character may suggest others, and in turn, situations in which they can be placed. Since you are limited in how much you can present about a character, you should choose the most important traits to be depicted and concentrate on these. To do this it is often good practice to think of the characters in terms of their goals or motivations.

Although the major characters need full development, there is no need to develop fully the minor characters who are needed only to advance the plot. There may be danger in developing them fully as they may arouse too much interest on the part of the audience and so detract from the main elements of the play.

All characters are a combination of the typical and the unique. Generally, the more important the character to the action, the more of an individual that person should be.

Most of what is learned about a character in a play is learned because of his actions. The character should be placed in situations that best can reveal dominant personality traits. Suspense is held largely by revealing these traits of the characters. The climax of any play should be a logical outcome of the character's inherent makeup.

EXERCISES

1. Read a modern play and figure out everything you can about the background, physical aspects and personality of the central character. Has the playwright made the person believable? How could the character be better presented?

2. Read a play and determine the basic needs of the characters. Try to determine if these needs are logical.

3. Choose a tragedy and analyze the reasons for the central character's defeat.

4. Read a comedy and compare the central figure's dominant personality traits with the dominant traits of the central figure of the tragedy.

5. Read any modern play and determine to what extent the central character is both stereotyped and individualized.

6. Read a play in which there are several minor characters. Figure out why they are included and what part they play in the overall progression of the play.

7. Develop a character that could be the central figure in an original play. Write a detailed analysis of that character. Analyze goals, needs, drives and motives, as well as background, current situation, personality traits and physical appearance.

8. Develop two or three secondary characters who might react with the central character you have developed. Write an analysis of each.

9. Analyze the relationship among your characters and develop a situation in which you could place a combination of two or more of these characters.

1Ø. Write a scene based on the situation you have developed.

11. Write another scene that will effectively reveal an important trait of the central character.

12. Write a third scene that would be a logical outcome of one of the other two scenes you have written.

CHAPTER IV

THEME AND IDEA

Theme] is synonomous with idea. It's the play's purpose or what the writer wants to say to an audience. It doesn't have to be a profound discovery but can be merely a reexamination of something everyone knows. The playwright may simply want to restate a universal truth in order to reenforce it.

Theme is also tied closely to audience response. How does the playwright want the audience to feel after the final curtain? Why should they experience this feeling? Maybe the writer wants only to call attention to something important or worth remembering. Maybe he or she wants the audience to reexperience an awareness of a particular problem of society or to look more closely at their own values. Whatever the theme is, the audience will be more willing to accept the message of the play if they are in at least partial agreement with what the playwright wants to state. In this way, the writing of a play may be compared with a speech of persuasion in that the writer or speaker has a much better chance of reaching the audience by beginning with a common premise. For instance, if an audience didn't belive that war is wrong, an author would have little success in writing a play with an anti-war theme.

Often, theme is no more than an observation of life, rather than a concrete statement. The Absurdist dramatists, for example, state that life is absurd without trying to urge any point of view upon the audience. Often the playwright will only lead the audience in a particular direction rather than making a definite statement about any aspect of life. Such is the case with The Bald Soprano where Ionesco points up the lack of meaningful communication among people but doesn't suggest that this should or can in any way be changed. Writers thus sometimes allow the audience to interpret and to draw their own conclusions.

Too often playwrights attempt to "hit the audience" with a specific theme or viewpoint. But maybe the audience members don't agree with the point of view, or they feel they are being preached at rather than entertained. Audiences have to be made to feel; playwrights have to try to elicit certain responses, or else they may as well have had a soap box and given a speech.

A serious play appeals more to the audience's feelings of empathy. Viewers also probably will feel a wider range of emotions in connection with the characters or the situation, in contrast to their reactions in viewing a comedy. The latter appeals more to our intellects. It should make us feel, but the feelings will be tied in with happiness or laughter. The audience also should experience satisfaction. A treatise on Einstein's theory of relativity will appeal to the intellect, but it won't be funny.

The treatment of the subject matter often determines whether the play is comic or tragic. For example, consider Willy Loman's death as compared to the entire issue of death in the novel and movie, The Loved One. The latter presents a totally ludicrous picture or a mockery of our views of death.

Sometimes it's better to attempt to depict a character rather than trying consciously to dramatize a theme. Often the theme becomes apparent or is brought to life only after the other elements of the play are being developed. For example, if you start with a character you want to portray, you may discover that what the character says and does determines the theme. On the other hand, you may want to deal with a certain subject matter to bring it to the attention of the audience. Your feelings about the subject determine your approach to it, and in this way you will develop a theme.

Many authors probably do not begin with a particular message in mind. If they do, they have to be careful that the play doesn't become too rigid or artificial, or that the characters don't become paper-thin. An example of this type of writing is the thesis drama that was developed by such men as Alexander Dumas, fils, who wrote Camille. The aim was to teach a lesson or to correct a moral wrong. The stage became a pulpit from which the dramatists preached their own principles of morality. In fairness, it must be stated that the thesis play can be developed well and may be a strong form, as evidenced in some of the plays of Henrik Ibsen. Although they may be considered outdated in some respects, plays such as The Pillars of Society, A Doll's House and Ghosts, still have much to commend them. But most of us are not Ibsens and cannot make thesis drama work for us as well as he could.

DISCOVERING SUBJECT MATTER AND THEME

Perhaps you are the type of person, as most are, who believes you don't have anything to say to an audience. You may question what message you could have for others that they would want to spend more than two hours hearing. Maybe you feel you haven't lived long enough or haven't experienced enough to write anything worthwhile. Such feelings are common but not really justified. First, when it come to writing, you have two advantages, although they may seem to contradict each other. One is that your background and experiences are different from those of anyone else. The other is that your background and experiences are similar to those of others.

How can these two things help you in your writing? To appeal to an audience, a play must have elements which are recognizable. There has to be a common ground upon which the audience and the playwright meet. Even if you live in California, you have much in common with a person who lives in Rhode Island. American citizens experience emotions similar to those felt by Japanese citizens. No human being is totally alien to any other human being. We all experience the feelings of anger, love hatred, disgust and fear. We've all been in similar situations. We've been ill or in pain. We've all experienced loss and rejoiced with others over their good fortune. We've all been jealous of another's achievements. "There's nothing new under the sun" is true in that every emotion that can be felt by a human being probably has been felt. For every situation or every action that is taken there have been similar situations or similar actions. What you've experienced in your lifetime has been experienced by others at many times and in many places. Psychologists say that human beings learn by relating new situations and encounters to what they already know. They build upon previous knowledge. In this way their universe is expanded. It's rare to encounter something entirely outside your realm of experience or knowledge.

Audiences in a theatre relate the action on the stage to their own backgrounds and personalities. Just as children learn by watching others, so do audiences learn through observations. Both theatre and life are related in a large degree to humankind's mimetic instinct. But there would be no such thing as a mimetic instinct if there were no need to relate

41

others' actions to our own lives. We do all share common experiences and common goals.

Conversely, the chain of events that makes up your life differs from that of anybody else. Your perceptions of the world and your interpretation of events are slightly different in some cases and vastly different in others to anyone else's views of the same things. That accounts in part for the difficulty policemen often have in obtaining a description of a robber. Each witness describes the person differently. Our mental attitudes color our perceptions.

In one of the stories in <u>Welcome</u> <u>to</u> <u>the</u> <u>Monkey</u> <u>House</u> Kurt Vonnegut, Jr., writes about a society in which there were attempts to make everyone equal by handicapping those individuals who had outstanding abilities or attributes in any one area. Thus the handsome or beautiful were masked, and the intelligent had their thoughts interrupted electronically. The physically strong had to carry added weight, and the television announcers had speech problems. The idea of such a society appears ridiculous to us. We need a sense of personal identity. We want to be recognized for our outstanding qualities, while on the other hand, we don't want to stand out because of any defect. No matter what the basis for consideration, no one person is exactly the same as any other. It is these differences that provide interest for the audience. Therefore, when choosing ideas for a play, you have to have a balance between what is common to everyone in the audience and what is unique to the individual.

The individuality of your background and perceptions will hold an audience's attention. The same thing will allow you to present something a little differently than it can be presented by someone else while making a common or universal statement. Whether you want to entertain, to make the audience aware of something or to present a unique approach to an old idea, you can do it through writing.

You have experienced childhood and have grown through adolescence to adulthood. Perhaps the maturation process can provide you with subject matter or a theme for a play. If you had the time, you could write literally dozens of plays concerned with growing up.

You could deal with specifics or present an

ecclectic view of your childhood and adolescence. You could try just to recapture a particular period as was done by the authors of the musical, Grease, which did little more than present a facet of teenage life in the fifties. Compare the musical Annie, based on the comic strip, Little Orphan Annie with The Miracle Worker or The Diary of Anne Frank. The Miracle Worker is much more specific in its focus on the relationship between Helen Keller and her teacher, Annie Sullivan, and so is The Diary of Anne Frank, which is based on an actual journal written by a teenager forced to hide in an Amsterdam attic to escape the Nazis.

Your views of childhood differ greatly from these. But what can you possibly say personally about growing up? Start with an examination of your attitudes about your own childhood. Do you view it with nostalgia? Are you bitter about the way you were treated by your parents? What provided the highlights or the biggest disappointments?

You have only to look around you for all sorts of ideas. Look at people, events, institutions and attitudes, but examine them critically. Learn to analyze how you feel about the things you encounter in everyday life. Part of the success in writing is living up to the old maxim: "Know thyself." In their book, The Writer's Survival Guide, Jean and Veryl Rosenbaum talk about examining your psychohistory as a means of knowing self and so being able to use this knowledge in writing. This means asking yourself questions similar to those you asked when developing a character. As the Rosenbaums state on Page 71, "You will discover a more spontaneous recall if you respond to the questions with feelings rather than intellect." You begin asking yourself questions about your earliest childhood and advance through later life. This helps you know and often understand feelings and thus you have material for your writing.

Once you learn to evaluate and examine your own life, you will have a better idea of what you can write. Your approach or the way you feel will determine the kind of play. Is there something you want to ridicule? Or should the same subject be treated in a light, humorous vein? Perhaps it demands a serious treatment. No matter what ideas or opinions you have, you can treat them in any number of ways.

OUR BASIC NEEDS

Another way of choosing a subject or theme for a play is to examine basic needs, those things that are necessary to sustain a reasonably happy life. Examine how they are stifled in everyday life, and again you have the basis for any number of plays. Many writers have examined the social environment of their time and come up with a play, whether the purpose was to bring a certain situation to light or to make mockery of it. Such diverse presentations resulted as Gilbert and Sullivan's satire of the British navy in and Ibsen's dramatizations of women's oppression in , which deals with a woman being forced to live with the ghosts of her husband's past.

You can relate these basic needs to your own life. You have certain expectations. Sometimes you are opposed in attempting to make these expectations reality. How does this opposition affect you?

Basic needs include such things as security, recognition, response, adventure, worship and self-preservation. Let's examine some of these in detail. What types of security do people need? First, we need physical security. We want the law to protect us. We want to feel secure in knowing that if we step outside we won't be mugged. We want financial security. We need money for food, clothing and shelter, all basic necessities. We want to feel comfortable in social situations, and the security of good health. The list is almost endless.

Now, take one of these types of security and look at how it can be treated in a play. Take governmental security, which includes war themes. They range from to . The former, a comedy about World I by Stallings, Laurenceand Anderson, Maxwell was quite outspoken in its dialogue and authentic treatment of war. Gassner, John says it did more than any other dramatic piece to promote the cause of realism and freedom of speech on the American stage. The latter, a satire on soldiering, war and romantic melodrama, contains such characters as Captain Bluntschli who carries chocolates in his cartridge belt and a heroine who is an unconscionable liar.

Another need is for recognition, which also can take many forms. A person wants status, which can range from recognition of musical ability to success in business. Consider the woman who heads all the fund drives in her community to the neglect of her family and other interests. She may believe in the causes, but, on the other hand, her major motive may be to gain recognition by having others praise her "good works." An Academy Award winning film of a few years ago that dealt with the need for recognition was <u>Chariots of Fire</u>, which was about foot racing.

WRITE ABOUT WHAT YOU KNOW

Ideas are fleeting. You may be struck with one you like so much you think you cannot possibly forget it. But many times you will. Also, almost anything can start your mind working toward an idea that could be developed into a play. It could be overhearing a conversation, the way a person walks down the street or the appearance of someone's apartment. So you might try carrying a note pad and pencil with you and keeping a pen and paper beside your bed since many ideas come when you are most relaxed.

Ideas for a play may come from a situation, a bit of dialogue or a character. But it's a good idea to heed the old advice: "Write what you know." Stay within your own experience. What does this mean? Does it mean, if you have never been an uncle, you cannot write about uncles, or if you have never been a basketball player you cannot write about basketball players? Does it mean if you are a man, you cannot write a play whose central character is a woman? Of course not. If you were limited to what you have experienced personally, you could have only one character, or at most several variations of one character in every play.

Rather than just writing about what you've experienced, include things you've observed as well. But be sure you know enough about them to be convincing. If, for instance, you have never visited France, it would be foolish to write a play which was set in Paris. If your setting is New England in winter and you have never lived through a New England winter, you might not be convincing or credible. You may have visited that area of the country, but you probably should spend several winters there before you use such a setting as the basis of a play.

There are exceptions. If the setting is nonrealistic, then you are free to invent. Nobody can say any better than James Hilton what Shangrai La is like. Moss hart remarked in his autobiography, <u>Act One</u>

One, that he deliberately chose settings that were unfamiliar to him because then he could be more imaginative. But if a writer does this, there's the risk of having some glaring inconsistencies. Sometimes research can make a play seem authentic. This would apply to plays dealing with a particular historical period. It would be impossible to observe first-hand how conditions were at the time the action is to have taken place.

The Pulitzer Prize-winning playwright Paul Green relied largely upon research in writing his play, Trumpet in the Land, first produced in 1970. The play takes place during the late eighteenth century, so Green could not know first-hand about the situations and conditions of the time. But there were numerous documents that described those conditions. Not only did the playwright investigate these documents, but also he spent a great deal of time in Tuscarawas County, Ohio, where most of the action of the play occurs.

A common mistake is not checking out everything of a factual nature before including it in a play. If the locale is New York City at the present time, the playwright has to know about the city. He cannot place buildings and streets where he wants them. If one of the characters in the play refers to a real person, the material that is stated must be true. You cannot change laws or misquote facts to suit your purpose. In the framework of your play you can establish circumstances where facts can be distorted, but the audience must recognize this as a part of the framework. If you're unsure of your facts, either look them up or don't include them. If you're doing a historical play, begin with research. If you're writing about a particular area or a particular group of people, learn about that area or those people.

You should have little trouble if you do write what you know because, at best, the only thing you can do is to state recognized themes or ideas in a new way, or from a slightly different point of view. It's been said that there are only three basic plots that are used over and over again. Perhaps this statement is a little too restrictive, but it does illustrate a point. Although a play in finished form is unique, the playwright should not waste time worrying whether the basic ideas or the theme is unique. If either were, the play probably would be too far removed from an audience's frame of reference for them to gain anything from it.

DETERMINING THEME THROUGH SELECTIVITY

One way to look at the process of writing is as an interpretation of life. Playwrights can make statements, can call attention or can make people aware of things they have failed to see. They can try to bring about a reformation of social problems, but they must remember that what they are asking is based on the way they see something or on their interpretation of existing conditions. That's why there are such diverse plays about war as <u>Arms</u> <u>and</u> <u>the</u> <u>Man</u> and <u>What</u> <u>Price</u> <u>Glory?</u>

Dramatists, through selectivity, place importance only on what they consider to be important. They exaggerate; they ignore other viewpoints by condensing time and action, by emphasizing character traits and by editing dialogue. There's nothing wrong with this; it's what human beings do all the time. But playwrights must make it work for them. They must be selective in including only what they want to say to express a theme or to get across a character. In effect, playwrights should write the way they feel. Although they should never fail to recognize that other people view things differently than they do, they should be able to stand up for their viewpoints. Just as others are free to persuade us, we are free to convince them that ours is the right interpretation.

Much of the credit for influencing the start of naturalistic drama has been given Emile Zola. Those writing in the style he advocated believed that a play should be only an observation of life. A playwright's task was to record faithfully all details of action, character and setting. The writer was to build no climax nor emphasize any element of the play more than another. It was felt that to plan a beginning or an ending to a play was not being truthful since in real life there is no beginning or end. Everything that the writer observed was included with nothing stressed or emphasized.

Such a "slice of life" play had no real theme. It could say nothing to an audience except that "this is a segment of one type of life." Today's audience would find such a form, if presented regularly, boring and monotonous. For example, go to a party sometime and try to record the conversation for two hours without saying anything yourself. Observe everything that

47

people say and do. You will find that the whole thing seems almost ludicrous, and you will probably wonder how the people themselves can find any enjoyment in the situation.

Today's writers have to interpret and select. Even if they allow their characters to take the action of the play into their own hands, the mind of the writer will blot out much of the inconsequential detail before it reaches the paper. More than that, playwrights can revise, change and heighten during the second or third drafts. It usually is better to have things to cut out of a play after the first draft than to have underwritten it. The danger in trying to add elements to each scene is that it forces words into the mouths of the characters or forces action. This can result in a feeling of artificiality. Adding a new scene is not such a risk because the characters can do as they please in the new situation.

If the first writing is too skeletal in nature, there's a danger of its becoming too analytical in the rewriting. Even in a comedy, the humor generally grows out of the situation or the characters themselves rather than out of a conscious attempt on the part of the playwright to write a joke. Such efforts often make the humor come across as a manufactured product.

You've probably seen productions in which too much manufacturing was done by the writer. You can find such situations in a host of contemporary non-royalty plays. Most audiences are too sophisticated to want to sit and watch such nonsense. Even if playwrights have to start out in an artificial manner by establishing their characters in a particular set of circumstances, they should let them work themselves out of the situation without intervening.

What has all the preceding to do with theme? First, if the audience feels the theme is being forced upon them, they are likely to respond by disgust or dislike. Second, if the play appears to them as artificial, they may begin to think that the writer lacks skill in putting it together and that he or she has nothing of value to say. If you see a person who's sloppily dressed, you begin to assess the person's character as sloppy. If you see a play that's poorly constructed, you likewise will begin to believe certain things about it that the playwright did not intend. Appearances can be deceiving. The person who is sloppily dressed may be highly intelligent; the play

that is sloppily constructed may have a theme or ideas
to commend it.

SUMMARY

Theme has to do with the playwright's purpose in
writing. It's what he or she wants to say to an
audience, whether it's a statement, an impression or
just a view of life.

Your own unique background and experiences,
through similar to others, are what give you the basis
for beginning to write. They are what maintain
interest and make your writing or your style different
from everyone else's. It's impossible to come up with
anything entirely new. The best you can hope to do is
to present old ideas or concepts in a slightly
different light.

Themes or ideas can come from almost anywhere.
You should learn to be conscious of potential ideas by
evaluating your environment. Other ideas for a play
can come from an examination of humanity's basic
needs. If one of these needs is thwarted or stifled,
there is conflict and struggle on the part of the
character.

It usually is best not to begin a play with a
theme. Begin with other elements and the theme will
develop. If you start with a theme and not with a
character or a situation, the play may not come across
well to an audience. In addition, you have to know
about the experiences and the settings you want to
include in the play to make it authentic. You should
write about what you know either through experience or
observation. The writing should be backed by solid
research.

Writing a play is, in effect, interpreting life.
Playwrights select what they consider to be important.
They heighten and thus better express their viewpoint,
without considering whether it is in opposition to
other people's perceptions of the world. This is what
gives the play its theme and brings out its important
ideas. In accomplishing this purpose the writer should
not force situations and dialogue upon the actors but
should let events occur naturally.

EXERCISES

1. Read both a modern play and an Elizabethan play

and determine the theme or purpose of each. Judge their effectiveness.

2. Read a tragedy or a serious play and evaluate its potential for audience identification and empathy.

3. Read any other play and discuss its effectiveness in terms of audience response.

4. Choose two possible areas of subject matter from your own background that could be used as the basis of a play.

5. Analyze how one of these instances from your background could be developed into a play. How would you present the subject matter?

6. Take one of humankind's basic needs and formulate a situation that could be the basis of a play. Relate one of these needs to the central character you developed after reading Chapter III.

7. Read a historical play and judge how effectively it conveys the overall feeling of the period.

8. Choose any play and attempt to discover a method of logically changing its outcome.

9. Write a "slice of life" scene you have observed. Now make it more effective dramatically.

10. Compare the effectiveness of the action in a modern non-royalty play with the effectiveness of the action in a royalty play. What are the strong and weak points of each?

CHAPTER V

DIALOGUE

There are three important aspects of dialogue: clarity, appropriateness and naturalness. If there is any overriding or common weakness most beginning playwrights have, it's the writing of dialogue, which often becomes stilted, stuffy and forced. Since most plays are representational, that is, they attempt to present the actors as real people in real situations, the dialogue has to sound much like ordinary, everyday speech.

What is meant by this? There is no clear-cut definition. Nobody speaks in exactly the same manner as any other person. People in one part of the country have slightly different vocal patterns and inflections than those in other parts. Expressions heard in one place may be unusual in another. Even people who grew up in the same area and have similar backgrounds speak differently. How then can the author determine just what is natural and appropriate? First, the dialogue must be natural to the character. How would such a character speak? Why would the person speak in a certain way? Many answers can be determined by the character analysis discussed in Chapter III. If the character is a stuffy person, he or she will speak in a more formal, stilted manner than will an uninhibited, outgoing character, even though the same nuances of dialect may be present in the speech of both. The dialogue should fit the personality of the character and thus help reveal the type of person he or she is.

Environment also determines in part the way a character speaks. Many American-born residents of New York's Chinatown speak English with a Chinese accent. This is natural because they imitate the speech patterns of their parents and relatives. It's not at all unusual for a child to use the same vocal quality as the parent. If the parent's voice has a whining quality, the child's voice also may take on that characteristic. It's common for a northerner to live in the south for a few months and acquire a southern accent while still retaining some of his or her former speech characteristics.

The extent of one's schooling often determines certain speech habits. If for some reason a person had to drop out of school after a few years, his or her

51

grammar may not be as good as that of a person with more extensive schooling, nor may the person have the background to express thoughts as coherently as a person with more formal education. Just as much can be told by the way characters look and act, much also can be inferred from the way they speak.

LEARNING TO HEAR SPEECH PATTERNS

With practice the writing of dialogue will take care of itself in the matter of style, if you have a clear idea of your characters. One of the best ways of learning to write believable dialogue is learning to hear it. Try to figure out why one person talks differently from another. Part of the first impression you gain of people is from their speech. Analyze what makes you conclude certain things about them, and then try to figure out if the conclusions are justifiable.

Writing down what you hear in different situations can help you begin to understand speech patterns and how they are used. Try recording conversations among college students having a bull session, between two workers coming home on a bus or between two old women out for a day of shopping.

Then take the conversations and try to extend them, using the same vocal patterns and style that you've recorded. The two women shoppers may be complaining about high prices. Try to figure out why. Are they on fixed incomes? Are they complaining because they cannot afford some of the luxuries they would like, or is it only that such complaints are expected as a part of passing the day? Maybe they feel that such a subject is safe ground. If they talk about prices, they don't have to reveal their personalities. They can speak about something that <u>seems</u> important in order to avoid something that <u>is</u>.

When you are extending the conversation, try to imagine the actions that go along with the words. What facial expressions and body movements are used? These also can tell a great deal about a person's character and the way he or she is feeling. Such practice helps both in writing accurate, believable dialogue and in the development of character. It even may give you ideas for a play.

DIFFERENCES BETWEEN CONVERSATION AND DIALOGUE

It would be impractical to transfer actual conversation to the stage. First, dialogue needs to be selective. Most conversations tend to ramble and change directions. They often are social in nature and thus inconsequential. People want to have contact with one another, but they know there are limitations in such contact and don't want to run the risk of being rebuffed or rejected by stating their feelings. Yet they want to feel a part of the whole. They want to feel they matter, so they compromise and talk to each other about trivial things.

On the stage dialogue has to have a purpose. Even when the main point of a particular play is lack of communication, the dialogue has to be selective. Eugene Ionesco's The Bald Soprano takes the everyday lack of awareness and makes it appear more absurd than it is. People usually are able to recognize their husbands or wives, and they don't become shocked over someone's tying a shoe lace, as the couples do in Ionesco's play.

Dialogue makes a point. It's not as repetitive as normal conversations where words, phrases and ideas may be repeated several times. Unless the situation demands it, or it is for emphasis or character portrayal, dialogue is much less redundant than everyday speech. This is so in order to establish a character quickly and advance the plot.

RULES OF WRITING DIALOGUE

A play is not the place for writers to show off their vocabularies or to use flowery language. Forced cleverness tends to grate on the nerves of the audience. The dialogue becomes unnatural and artificial. On the other hand, all the rules of dialogue can be forgotten if their violation is important in establishing or portraying character. A writer once was criticized for using a cliche in one of his novels. He answered that although he never used such figures of speech himself, his characters certainly did. In other words, include the language that suits the character, but do not overdo it. The way a character speaks is established shortly after the first entrance. If the person's speech is filled with cliches, the audience will be able to recognize this without the playwright's driving the point home endlessly.

Unlike readers of a novel, the theatre audience doesn't have time to reflect upon each speech. Such reflection can come at the end of the play. But if there's too much necessity for it throughout, the audience won't be able to keep up with the action. That is not to say that a play need deal with shallow subject matter or circumstances, but only that the playwright avoid intricate phrasing and sentence structure. The audience must be able to grasp the meaning.

The language and speech have to be clear so the audience can easily understand what the characters are saying, even if they use improper grammar or speak with an accent. For one thing, this involves using fairly simple sentences, rather than those that are long and involved. Besides being easier for the audience to grasp, they also are easier for actors to memorize and deliver. And, of course, dialogue should avoid tongue twisters, unless they are included for a particular, comic effect. Dialogue needs to avoid ambiguities and be easily interpreted and understood. The lines should be coherent, leading directly from one thought or idea to another.

There should be a natural rhythm and flow to the language of a play. It has to help establish mood and atmosphere and advance the plot toward a climax. As such, it should fit the emotional content of the scenes and the emotions of the characters. Usually, the more passive the emotion, the longer and smoother the sentences and speeches. The higher the emotional pitch, the more staccato and abrupt the dialogue. In this way dialogue corresponds to real life situations.

Think of a time when you were upset and angry. Suppose you got into a quarrel with a friend or relative. Try to remember how you expressed yourself. If you were in a rage, you probably become almost inarticulate, or you may have slowed your rate excessively and articulated very clearly. Now think of a time when you were feeling contentment. How did this emotion affect the way you spoke?

Long speeches often serve no useful purpose and slow down the action. There are exceptions as can be seen by reading the poetic dialogue of many of Eugene O'Neill's characters. But most playwrights probably would not be able to hold an audience's attention if they wrote speeches of comparable length.

Another reason to avoid long speeches is that the major device for advancing a plot is action, which implies reaction and interaction. If one character is forced to stand and listen while another makes a long speech, how can the person effectively portray his or her personality for an audience? Long speeches become repetitive as well as monotonous. During some periods of theatrical history, they were expected. But today's audiences are not as willing to accept them.

Dialogue has to hold the audience's interest. It needs to be concrete and should not call attention to itself.

PURPOSES OF DIALOGUE

Dialogue has several purposes besides holding interest and attention. First, it gives information essential to each scene and to the play as a whole. Other than through the technical aspects of a production, it's the only way that expository material can be delivered. The playwright has to be certain that such exposition doesn't intrude upon the logical progression of the scene. It has to fit the context of the play and not stand out. The audience needs to receive information without being aware that they have received it. A certain amount of exposition is essential to an understanding of any play, but it must be skillfully handled and worked into the dialogue so that it seems natural. Consider, for instance, the following brief scene from Oscar Wilde's The Importance of Being Earnest.

ALGERNON: How are you, my dear Earnest? What brings you up to town?

JACK: Oh, pleasure, pleasure! What else should bring one anywhere? Eating as usual, I see, Algy!

ALGERNON: (Stiffly) I believe it is customary in good society to take some slight refreshment at five o'clock. Where have you been since last Thursday?

JACK: (sitting down on the sofa) In the country.

ALGERNON: What on earth do you do there?

55

JACK: (pulling off his gloves) When one is in town one amuses oneself. When one is in the country one amuses other people. It is excessively boring.

ALGERNON: And who are the people you amuse?

JACK: (airily) Oh, neighbours, neighbours.

ALGERNON: Got nice neighbours in your part of Shropshire?

JACK: Perfectly horrid! Never speak to them.

ALGERNON: How immensely you must amuse them! (Goes over and takes a sandwich) By the way, Shropshire is your county, is it not?

JACK: Eh? Shropshire? Yes, of course. Hallo! Why all these cups? Why cucumber sandwiches? Why such reckless extravagance in one so young? Who is coming to tea?

ALGERNON: Oh! merely Aunt Augusta and Gwendolen.

JACK: How perfectly delightful!

ALGERNON: Yes, that is all very well; but I am afraid Aunt Augusta won't quite approve of your being here.

JACK: May I ask why?

ALGERNON: My dear fellow, the way you flirt with Gwendolen is perfectly disgraceful. It is almost as bad as the way Gwendolen flirts with you.

JACK: I am in love with Gwendolen. I have come up to town expressly to propose to her.

ALGERNON: I thought you had come up for pleasure? . . . I call that business.

JACK: How utterly unromantic you are!

ALGERNON: I really don't see anything romantic in proposing. It is very romantic to be in love. But there is nothing romantic about a definite proposal. Why, one may be accepted. One usually is, I believe. Then the excitement is all over. The very essence of romance is uncertainty. If ever I get married, I'll certainly try to forget the fact.

A great deal of information is given the audience here, in a very entertaining way. First, we can surmise that Jack and Algernon are friends---fairly close since Jack has apparently dropped in unexpectedly. We can tell quite a bit about the social standing of the two. We know that Algernon is soon going to serve tea to Gwendolen and his aunt. We learn that Jack probably loves Gwendolen and the feelings are reciprocated. We learn something about the men's views, and seeds are planted for future events and conflicts. For example, we can suppose that there is going to be a scene in which Aunt Augusta and Jack are in opposition.

Wilde also knew what he was doing in presenting the scene through a series of conflicts and disagreements. Rather than Jack's merely entering and talking about where he's been and then Algernon stating that the two other characters will be arriving, all of this is brought out in a series of small disagreements which, though not at all serious, do maintain our interest. For example, Algernon is somewhat accusatory in asking where Jack has been. Then through his line, "What on earth do you do there?" we can infer that he doesn't particularly like the country. The lines are humorous also because they are unexpected. After Jack says that he amuses the neighbors, it's natural to think that he likes them. But then he says they are "horrid." All of this reveals not only the setting, including place, financial status, and so on, but a great deal about the kind of people Jack and Algernon are.

Dialogue advances the theme of the play. Largely through what is said, an audience is able to tell what direction the play is taking. We can surmise from the excerpt from The Importance of Being Earnest that the play will be a drawing room comedy, and that the characters and situation are not to be taken

seriously. We also can see that the theme probably
will have something to do with romance or love. Like
exposition, theme should not call attention to itself
but should be transmitted to the audience only in terms
of the overall plot. Yet those portions of the play
that contain the most important information have to be
written clearly and precisely as part of the total
play.

Through a combination of dialogue, setting and
treatment of subject matter the audience learns the
overall mood or atmosphere of a play. Through the
language, the sentence structure and the interaction of
the characters the audience should be able to tell if
the scene is comic or tragic, nostalgic or mocking.
Changes in mood from scene to scene also can become
apparent through the use of dialogue, as well as
through the turn of events.

BUILDING SUSPENSE AND INTENSITY

A play has to build. Too many important elements,
too much background information, too much
intensification in a single speech are wrong. First,
except when delivering a speech or lecture, people
don't usually impart a lot of information in a single
exchange, so to do so in a play would sound unnatural.
Second, you have a play's entire structure to develop
plot, to heighten moments of tension, to build suspense
and to reveal character. Even expository material
doesn't have to be given all together. You cannot ask
the audience to absorb too much at once or they will
lose interest. Audiences don't want to work at
understanding the elements of the play. They want the
work done for them.

In conversation and in life there is a natural ebb
and flow. Such should be the case both with the
dialogue and with the action of a play. Even when two
people are in a lengthy, heated quarrel, the emotions
don't remain at one pitch of intensity. The characters
become angry, lose some of their anger and then become
more intense than previously. Such a scene has to
build to a peak and then fall off again. Intense
emotion cannot be maintained for a long period of
time. Carrying the dialogue at too high an emotional
pitch throughout a scene can have one of two effects.
Either the audience will become too emotionally drained
to be able to follow the action, or, more likely, they
will have no frame of reference for the intensity. It
loses its meaning. There's no way to build further,

and there's the likelihood that the scene will appear flat. Intensity has to be highlighted if it's to have meaning.

You may have a favorite food, but if you are forced to consume the same food day after day, meal after meal, it won't long remain a favorite. Many an actor has experienced starting a scene too high and finding that when it is necessary to build even further, there's no place to go. Such also is the case with writing. Contrasts are needed for emphasis. If a character attacks, he or she then retreats and attacks again. This gives the scene more impact, and the final attack more power. A play is a series of small climaxes building to a single large climax. The entire play has to be structured as the individual scenes, with some at a higher emotional pitch than others.

It's just as bad to have a scene change emotions too quickly or too often. What is supposed to be serious will appear only as funny. A large part of playwriting is tied to audience response. If the audience is confused about the kind of response expected, you have defeated your purpose. For example, suppose you have written a play. You submit it to a community theatre to be considered for production. You know you don't have much chance of having it selected because there are twenty other submissions, many of them from more experienced playwrights.

Still, you have some hope that your play will be chosen. Lo and behold, on the day the winning play is to be announced, you receive a phone call from the president of the community theatre telling you that you have won. You hang up the phone, almost in a state of shock. A few seconds later the phone rings again. You pick up the receiver. The person at the other end tells you that your brother has been critically injured in a traffic accident. How do you react? You want to be happy, but you feel guilty about it. The point is that you should rarely put your audience into the same quandry. If you do, they may just want to retreat from the emotions altogether.

PHYSICAL ACTIVITY

Pantomime or physical activity, exclusive of conversation, can be just as effective or at times more effective than dialogue. For example, consider the success of such plays as Children of a Lesser God or The Miracle Worker, both of which have deaf characters

59

who do not or cannot speak.

If characters become frustrated or angry, let the audience see them venting their emotions rather than talking about them. If characters fall in love, rather than having them deliver a speech extolling the wonders of the emotion, show the audience how they react to their discovery and how they treat the persons they love.

Physical action, as well as dialogue, has to be appropriate. If the characters are in a state of mild anxiety or tension, they may fuss with little details in the set. They may straighten pictures, shift magazines on a coffee table or constantly readjust their costumes. On the other hand, if they are experiencing strong anxiety, the actions are stronger. The characters may pace quickly, slam a fist into things or make other broad, quick movements. You don't have to plan out every detail of movement, but you should be able to visualize the characters in action. Just as you would not force dialogue upon the characters in order to control the direction of a scene, neither should you force physical action upon them. The action has to grow out of the character and like the pattern of speaking be appropriate to the personality. It's also a good idea to remember that characters onstage should have something to do or say. If they have long periods of silence or inactivity, there probably is little purpose in having them in the scene. Actors with nothing to do also will begin to feel uncomfortable.

IDENTIFYING WITH YOUR CHARACTERS

To a large extent the characters take care of themselves in the matter of development, dialogue and action. But you have to become involved with what they are doing or saying because when it comes right down to it, the playwright is the person doing the speaking. In effect, the writer becomes each character in much the same way an actor becomes a character when involved with a role. It is next to impossible to establish credibility or to present three-dimensional characters whose dialogue and actions are believable, if you cannot identify with them. In The Writing of One Novel: The Prize, Irving Wallace says that when he stops writing to eat dinner with his family, he often is somewhat shocked not to see his characters sitting around the table. He has identified so closely with them that they have become real people. The same thing has to happen with any writer who wants to present characters realistically.

REVISING THE DIALOGUE

After the dialogue for a scene is written, the playwright's work is just beginning. Now you have to go through the scene to select and arrange the material. This is much more of a mechanical process than it is to allow the characters to speak and act for themselves. It's more of an intellectual exercise because you need to be aware of the technical aspects of structure, of developing sentences that make sense and of cutting out what is unnecessary.

You have to throw things out to heighten the effectiveness of the scene and possibly to interject dialogue needed for the audience's understanding. The task is hard because you have to be completely analytical about it while at the same time retaining the feeling of the scene. If dialogue has to be added, you need to make certain that it fits into the style of the scene and that it meshes with the way the characters are expressing themselves.

The next job is to judge the overall effectiveness of the dialogue. Does it portray personality as well as it should? Does it sound as natural as possible? Does it suit the character and the way the person is feeling in each specific instance? Often it's a good idea to read the entire play aloud to see if the dialogue does adhere to spoken language and doesn't sound more formal that it should. Both by reading it aloud yourself and having others read it so you can just concentrate on listening, you can more easily judge its effectiveness. Many things that seemed all right as written may now sound awkward or stilted. The spoken word, even in formal situations, is actually far less formal than is the written word. There is less importance put on sentence structure and less attention called to slight errors in grammar. Slang terms are used more often in speaking than in writing, although you should be careful about using such terms in your play in that many are easily outdated. For instance, it now sounds pretty strange to our ears to hear all the "swells" that are scattered throughout many movies of the forties.

Another problem is that of describing moods and feelings. A writer of fiction can add such things as "oh, yes," he laughed, he joked, he cried. The playwright cannot communicate sentences such as: In a harsh voice Ruth sneered, "Get out of my life!" Of course, you can include such things as part of the stage directions, but in most cases this shouldn't be necessary. The feelings and style of delivery intended should be apparent from the content of the scene. A good rule to follow is that whenever stage directions of this sort can be omitted, omit them. Not only will it keep you on your toes as a writer in making sure you are communicating what you want, but it will allow the actor more freedom of interpretation. If the scene is well written and if the mood or atmosphere is conveyed through the sense of the action, you can be fairly certain that the lines will be delivered effectively.

SOME FINAL RULES

There are some additional rules to remember about writing dialogue. First, it's more powerful to speak in the active voice than the passive. It's better to say, "He threw the ball through the window," than to say, "The ball was thrown through the window." Generally, you should avoid "ing" words because they lack power. "When I saw the doctor, he said I have to go into the hospital," is somewhat better than, "Having gone to the doctor, I was told that I have to go into the hospital." The sentence can be further improved: "The doctor said I have to go into the hospital." Obviously, if a physician told someone to go into the hospital, the person had to have contact with the doctor to be told. It becomes a matter of getting to the point as quickly as possible, which often means the sentence becomes more powerful. Usually, is is better to omit a great many adjectives and adverbs. Compare "I really and truly want, more than anything, to get that great job, and I'll try as hard as I can to get it," to "I want that job, and I'll get it." Although it isn't stated in the second sentence that the speaker will try for the job, the implication is more powerful than the actual statement. Nor is it stated that the job is "great." But it is implied in the fact that the speaker wants it.

Characterization still should override other considerations. If the person is the type who would avoid the point, or if the situation demands dialogue that does not follow a straight line, you should write accordingly.

In writing dialogue remember that one speech usually leads directly into the next. The changes

62

shouldn't be abrupt. There need to be transitions. You have to consider that almost every line is a cue line for another character. The lines have to be written so that each character has motivation for responding, or the dialogue will sound choppy.

SUMMARY

The most important aspects of dialogue are clarity, appropriateness and naturalness. Dialogue has to get to the point quickly and be free of repetition and extraneous detail. It has to fit the personality and mood of the speaker to sound believable.

The playwright has to take into consideration the background, environment and personality of the character to consider how the person would speak in each situation. A help in learning to write dialogue is to record actual conversations, after which you can take the dialogue and try to extend it. You also can judge how to heighten dialogue in a play by attempting to heighten that heard in everyday conversations. Although the dialogue onstage has to sound natural, it's different from conversation in that it usually is more purposeful and follows a particular direction more than does most conversation. You should avoid flowery or stilted language unless it helps depict character. Long speeches usually should be avoided because they slow down the action.

Dialogue imparts essential information and establishes the mood of the play. Largely through dialogue, the theme of the play is set forth. You should be certain that no scene is kept at a high emotional pitch throughout, or the intensity will have no meaning. Part of the success of a play depends upon building suspense, and if too much material is included in one scene, there can be no suspense built as nothing important can be communicated later. There is a natural ebb and flow to conversations and to situations, and you should build the scenes and the play to conform to this rhythm. On the other hand, if you change emotional directions too quickly, the audience won't know how to react. Physical action is just as important or more important than dialogue in conveying essential information.

Once the first draft of the play is completed, there remains the task of heightening, selecting and arranging the dialogue. Finally, you must attempt to judge whether the dialogue effectively communicates the sense of the play and portrays character as well as it can.

1. Record three different conversations among people of differing backgrounds. What are the major differences in the way the people spoke, in the subject matter, in the language and in the direction of the conversation?

2. Write an analysis of a participant in one of the conversations you have recorded. Include what you know as well as what you can assume. On what basis were the assumptions made?

3. Record another conversation of approximately three minutes. On the basis of your impression of the participants extend the conversation another two minutes.

4. Make a recorded conversation more effective through selectivity.

5. Take the same conversation and, using all the techniques you can, make it more interesting and more dramatically effective.

6. Choose a scene from a published play. Slightly change the direction and the outcome by altering the dialogue.

7. Choose another scene from a published play and analyze the effectiveness of the dialogue. Determine if and how it could be improved.

8. Write a short section of dialogue in which one or more of the participants speaks with an accent.

9. Previously, you developed a central character and placed him or her in some scenes. Choose one of these scenes and rewrite the dialogue to make it more effective.

10. Write a short scene in which one or more traits of your central character are revealed largely through action, rather than through dialogue.

11. Write dialogue for a scene in which the central character you have developed is having a quarrel with another character.

12. Write another scene in which your central
    character is feeling happiness, frustration or
    anxiety.

CHAPTER VI

DRAMATIC STRUCTURE

So far you have read about where to get ideas for plays, about characterization, about dialogue and about theme. But how do these elements fit together? What is involved in the structure of a play?

Traditionally, theatre has dealt with the cause-to-effect play, which still draws the largest audiences so it is an excellent starting place for beginning playwrights. By exploring its structure first, you can learn all the elements of drama in a context that allows freedom but still establishes certain boundaries.

THE STORY PLAY

The cause-to-effect play can also be called the story play, the well-made play or the play with a plot. To call it the well-made play can be misleading since many people tend to look down upon a play of this name because it implies rigidity and artificiality. Many so-called "well-made" plays are in reality not made well at all since the action sometimes is forced and the climaxes lack proper motivation. It's really a matter of the connotations associated with the name. Perhaps cause-to-effect is better. A particular cause or set of causes brings about a specific effect or set of effects. As the name implies, there is no room for extraneous material. But it also could imply a skeletal plot in which a certain causal relationship is examined, much as a scientist puts a slide under a microscope for examination. So the name may connote something akin to a scientific study in which all human elements are recorded in an objective manner, which seems to exclude any sense of humanity or subjectivity on the part of the playwright.

It probably is better if the form is called the story play. From the time we are small, we learn to like stories. When we think of them, we generally think first of being entertained and second, perhaps, of learning something. Stories are interesting because they usually deal with people in situations with which we can identify. In books and plays our interest is maintained through our anticipation of the outcome and how it will be accomplished. A story holds our attention because of its unfolding and its revelations. In other words, the plot keeps us in suspense.

The plot of the story play involves the meeting of opposing forces. Their struggle continues until one of them is overcome. One is the protagonist, the other the antagonist. The former is the person who needs or wants something; the antagonist opposes him or her. The protagonist generally is an individual, though in rare cases it can be a group. The antagonist is another person, a group or a non-individualized force such as social or economic conditions. It may be the protagonist's environment, the forces of nature, or even a condition within the mind and is shown largely in the central character's relationships with other.

The story play begins with a particular situation in which there has been balance, or else the balance has been upset shortly before the action begins. At any rate, until the beginning of the action there has been no great difficulty for the characters. Then the inciting incident occurs and the balance is destoyed. A question is raised that must be answered. This introduces the rising action. During this period, the protagonist's problem is intensified through a series of complications. The suspense increases. Will the protagonist finally triumph or be defeated? The suspense, the struggle and the conflict continue to build until the action can go no further without something irrevocable happening. This means the turning point of the play has been reached. At this point the protagonist knows he or she will win the struggle against all opposition or else be destroyed. The actual point at which the central character wins or loses is the climax. The remainder of the play is devoted to the falling action, also called the denouement.

Sometimes the turning point and the climax are the same; at other times they are separated. Suppose two men are opposed. They have been fighting with each other because one man, the antagonist, has threatened the protagonist's family. After attempting to reason with the antagonist to no avail, the protagonist decides that the only solution is to kill the other man. The point at which the decision is made is the turning point. The actual killing is the climax. If the decision is carried out instantaneously, the turning point and the climax are the same. If the protagonist decides to kill the antagonist but feels it would be better to wait until a more opportune time, the turning point and the climax are separated.

In most plays, however, the action does not build in a straight line to the climax and then fall off for the unraveling or the reestablishment of the status quo. Instead the plot involves a jagged line where a series of minor crises and struggles are introduced as part of the overall problem. Sometimes these minor problems seemingly are resolved, only to intrude again and complicate the rising action. For example, in the musical, The Fantasticks, the first act ends with Matt and Luisa prepared to live happily ever after. But then the second act opens with each of them being dissatisfied with life, which each feels the need to experience further before settling down. So a problem---concerned with their spending the rest of their lives together---apparently has been solved by the end of the first act, only to be complicated further at the beginning of the second.

The complications in all but the simplest of stories result in a series of minor climaxes which could be compared to a fencing match. First, one person attacks and drives back the other; then the second attacks and drives back the first, over and over again at increasing intensity until one is declared the victor. Each of these minor crises somewhat alters the direction of the play. Each is introduced by one minor climax or resolution and ended by another. But the frenzy or suspense continues to build. It changes from speech to speech and from scene to scene.

Even in scenes where there appears to be no conflict, it is inherent; it relates to what already has been shown. Suppose a woman is having trouble at work. She is afraid of being fired even though she is the best worker on the job. Another worker tries to degrade everything she does and tries to take credit for everything worthwhile, thus making the woman look bad in the eyes of her boss. The woman comes into direct conflict with the villain at work. At home the situation appears to be calmer. Perhaps in discussing the situation with her husband, the woman decides what to do. The audience knows the conflict is present, that it's inherent in the action. It comes across indirectly in what the woman says and does.

Such a scene may validly be included in the script because it may show a part of the woman's character not apparent in her scenes with co-workers. It may reveal the inner workings of her mind and thus let the

69

audience know more about her. It may show what she is
planning to do and so build suspense or anticipation.
It makes the audience look forward to the confrontation
with the antagonist. Every scene of this nature must
relate to what already is known. It must not be
extraneous to the play, as, for instance, a scene of
the woman and her husband shopping would be. The scene
builds the audience's interest and further complicates
the plot. For example, Hamlet's well-known "To be or
not to be" soliloquy shows no direct action but only
what the character is thinking. Yet it does bear
directly on what he decides and also reveals many
facets of his character to us.

Plot refers to movement or progression and to
action. Without these, there would be little interest
in a play except possibly for the uniqueness or
originality of the setting or situation. But this
interest would rarely be great enough to be sustained
through a two-hour play. Action is what gives the play
its life.

DRAMATIC ACTION

There can be physical movement with no dramatic
action, as in the scene mentioned where a couple is
shopping. Such a scene often leads nowhere.
Conversely, there can be dramatic action without
physical movement. Such action is related to the
opposition of the protagonist and the antagonist in
moving the story forward. It needs to be motivated by
what has preceded it in the story.

A person planning how to thwart the attempts of
the antagonist to cheat him of an inheritance is using
dramatic action, though he may hardly move a muscle.
In another soliloquy, Hamlet decides when to kill his
uncle. He contemplates killing him at prayer, but
decides that then he would go to heaven. Instead, he
will kill him "when he is drunk asleep, or in his rage"
or at a similar time so "that his soul may be as damn'd
and black as hell."

This is not to imply that movement must be
restricted in any way simply because it does not seem
to contribute to the overall plot. Maybe it
accomplishes another valid purpose which indirectly
helps to advance the plot. Often, a character is
individualized in the eyes of the audience by some
repeated action. If she is a nervous person, perhaps
she plays with a ring or a strand of hair. Maybe a man

70

constantly refills and lights a pipe. Action such as this is valid in that it helps the audience to know the character better. It's an outward manifestation of an inner emotion or trait. The establishment of such a trait may be important to the later action.

Dramatic action must relate in some way to the central character. Even if this person isn't present, it must concern or be initiated because of him or her. To build the series of minor crises and climaxes that hold the interest of the audience, the central character must initiate action which in turn affects him or her. The characters in a play cannot be allowed to be unanswerable for what they do. Once they act, they must expect to be affected by their behavior. Dramatic action involves a clash of forces and is always reciprocal. It can be compared to communication. If you say hello to someone, that person usually says hello to you. If you argue with a friend, you can expect an argument back. But if you are talking to a group of people in a formal situation, they usually don't have the option of answering directly even though you do receive feedback in the form of facial expression and body language. The same thing occurs among characters in a play. For every action there has to be a reaction if the play is well-constructed. Nobody in a play is in his or her own personal limbo. All the major characters are responsible for everything they say and do.

Even when one character seems to dominate, there's an interchange of action. The other person is acting, through maybe not as forcibly. If this weren't so, or if there were no feedback, the play would lack meaning. Perhaps the person who is being dominated is slowly building up a resentment that will be acted upon later. For every moment after the initial balance is upset, there has be be action, whether it's the actual face-to-face meeting of opposing forces or action related to such a meeting.

Each minor complication or each change in action involves a revelation of character. We learn a little more about the central figure in a play by what he or she does when opposed. Therefore, the interest is further maintained.

The audience wants to know what the character really is like. Does the person live up to their expectations? Because of what the protagonist does, will he or she triumph? Or be defeated? How will this happen? Without dramatic action always occurring in the present tense, there would be no play. Although we learn a great deal about some of the other characters, including their motives, it's the central figure who must dominate. Every action that is taken, every scene that is included has to have direct bearing on whether this person will win or lose.

MAINTAINING AUDIENCE INTEREST

Plot is the arrangement of the dramatic action to build suspense and to reach a point of no return. As such, it must be probable and fit the play's framework. It has to be consistent with the personality of the character who performs the action and should be chosen to contribute to the overall effect of the play. We know because of the type character he is that Oedipus will continue on until he proves definitely who is the murderer of Laius. Such action is consistent with his character.

Interest also is maintained through selectivity. An action that would take longer in life can be compressed and heightened. Time can be condensed. Things can be accomplished more quickly and sentences formulated into a better structure on the stage, while still appearing or sounding natural. It would be rare indeed in real life to find any two people who have such a command of their language and thoughts under intense emotion as do George and Martha in Who's Afraid of Virginia Woolf?, where the scenes often become extremely intense.

Another way to maintain interest is through contrasts in the scenes, characters and actions.

The play also must have unity. One way it's provided is through the action being related to the struggle between the protagonist and the antagonist. There also is unity through the cause-to-effect relationship and the theme. A careful preparation for future events creates unity. Although some things may be unexpected, they are logical in the framework of the play. The action is organized and set forth to gain a specific unified response from the audience, whether it's to enrage them at some social ill, or to have them look at a style of living. But each action is motivated and each new situation should grow out of what has preceded it.

There is no particular length for each new

72

situation. Each may be a few lines or a few pages. When a climax is reached or an obstacle surmounted, a new situation is introduced. For example, a man is trapped in a burning building. He is first of all confronted by a door that won't open. When he manages to get the hinges off the door, he has met one crisis, but now he runs into the hallway where he is met by a wall of flame. He runs back into the room, grabs a blanket and wraps it around himself and rushes through the flames. A second problem has been met. Next he finds that the floor is crumbling beneath him, and so on. Although each problem is met and overcome, a new and worse one is introduced until the man either escapes or is overcome by the smoke and flames.

PROPORTIONING THE ACTS

Neither too much nor too little can be revealed in each act of your play. Too little will cause the play to lag; too much will leave nothing to maintain interest in succeeding acts or else will overwhelm the audience. By the end of the first act the audience should have all the background material necessary for an understanding of the play. For instance, in Ibsen's An Enemy of the People, though, of course, this is a five-act play, we know by the end of the first act how important the baths are to the economic survival of the town, and we can see the type of person Dr. Stockmann is. We know that he will try to have the baths shut down, and we know, because they disagree about so many things, his brother, the burgomaster, will oppose him. In other words, we see the entire conflict shaping up and we understand what is likely to happen and why. All the groundwork has been laid for the future.

This doesn't mean that there should be no exposition or revelation of character after the first act, but only that background material must have been given. Each of the first two acts should end on a high point to build audience anticipation for what is to follow.

Each act should end on a high emotional plane. Only if the spectators are involved in the story, only if they can empathize and identify with the major character will their attention be held. Writers and directors of movie serials of fifty years ago knew what they were doing when they ended one installment with the heroine strapped down and coming ever closer to the sharp teeth of the saw, or when a car containing the hero careened over a cliff just before "To be

73

continued" flashed on the screen. The audience knew that the heroine would be rescued and that somehow the hero would escape the smashed and burning automobile. But they didn't know how these things would be accomplished. The same should be true of a theatre audience at the end of the first two acts. The first act of West Side Story ends just after Bernardo of the Sharks, the Puerto Rican gang, stabs Riff of the Jets. Then Tony, the character based on Romeo, jumps forward and stabs Bernardo. Police whistles sound. The gangs disappear, except for Tony and a girl, Anybodys. She tries to pull Tony offstage. He finally realizes the danger he's in and manages to escape as a police search light cuts across the stage, making the ending extremely dramatic and intensely emotional.

It's probably best not to divide the acts into too many scenes where either a blackout or a curtain is required to show the passage of time or changes in the setting. If there are too many breaks of this sort, the play may begin to appear episodic and disconnected. There are times when it's necessary to have the act divided, but such a technique should be used sparingly. Some plays, of course, especially musicals, shift from one location to another quite often. The changes usually are worked out by the designer to take a minimum of time without any actual break in the action. The playwright should be aware of how such changes can be made and if they can fit the overall style of his play.

If the climax of the play is too early, the remaining scenes hold little interest. If it occurs too late, the audience may feel cheated because there may not be time for the "unraveling" and the reestablishment of the balance. Most often, the climax probably should come somewhere between the first third and the final third of the last act. If it's earlier, the remainder of the play may not hold the audience's attention. Also if the plot is so complicated as to warrant an early climax in order to explain all the events, it probably means that it was over-complicated and perhaps too difficult to follow. The only rule that can be set down is that the climax should be delayed as long as possible for suspense.

FALLING ACTION

After the climax should come the falling action, that part of the play that shows the results of the previous action. The climax begins to show the answer

74

to the question asked when the problem was introduced; the falling action finishes answering the question. It may answer more fully how and why a certain thing happened. It may show the effects of the resolution on the characters. At any rate, it ties up all the loose ends. The central character should be totally responsible for the specific outcome of the play. Therefore, if the play is a comedy and the protagonist is triumphant, the audience wants to enjoy the triumph with the character. If the protagonist is defeated and dies, the audience wants to feel the emotions felt by the other characters in the play.

For example, a man becomes separated from his family during wartime. The separation is the inciting incident. As soon as he is able, he begins searching for his wife and daughters. It may take years of following false leads. Throughout the action, the audience through empathy and identification has experienced the man's fears, his apprehensions, his despair and the fruitless bursts of hope. Finally, he discovers a promising clue and follows through with it. It leads to the climax of the play, the finding of his family. He knews he has reached his goal. He rushes to the house where they are staying and flings open the door. The problem has been resolved and the action completed. But since the audience has suffered with the man, they want to rejoice with him. They want to feel his happiness and witness the reunion. It would be poor writing to end the play at this point since it would in effect be cheating the audience members.

There are several specific points to keep in mind about structure in a story play. The first involves the type of opposition. There are five different types. They are the protagonist against: (1) **another person**, (2) **self**, (3) **society**, (4) **nature** and (5) **fate**. An example of the first is the play Sleuth, a two-character melodrama in which the two men constantly try to outwit each other and gain the upper hand. Often this type of play, though encompassing various genres, is simpler in plot and may not probe the protagonist's character so deeply as would be the case in plays with other types of opposition. An example of the second type is Death of a Salesman, in which Willy Loman tries to live up to his own definition of success. Many of Ibsen's plays are examples of a human being against society. A good example is Ghosts in which society forced Mrs. Alving to remain with a totally dissolute husband. Then after his death, she builds an orphanage to honor him and so hide his true character. But all her efforts to escape Alving fail in that her son, Oswald, has inherited a venereal disease from his father.

Although not a play, an excellent example of a human being against nature is Jack London's short story, "To Build a Fire," in which a man is trapped in freezing temperatures and tries to light a fire so he won't freeze to death. Often, this type of plot is difficult to write in that it comes across as too melodramatic. Many times in plays that pit a person against a force of nature, the conflict only superficially is between the protagonist and the force. Often it's the man or woman against self in the reaction to the flood or drought.

The fifth type of opposition is equally difficult to make convincing in that it often comes across as the protagonist's being controlled by fate without any sense of freedom. Superficially, Who's Life Is this Anyway, which deals with the right-to-die issue, is based on a protagonist versus fate in that the leading character is dying. But it's really a struggle against society, or accepted standards. Oedipus Rex also seems to be man against fate, but this is a matter of interpretation. If we view the Oracle's prophecy that Oedipus will kill his father and marry his mother as absolute truth, of course, this denies any freedom of choice. But we can also view what the Oracle says only as a prediction. Thus if Oedipus had followed the golden mean and not been excessively unreasonable, the prophecy would not have been fulfilled. If we take the former view of the play, it's certainly a plot of man against overwhelming fate. But if we choose the latter interpretation, the opposition involves Oedipus more completely against himself---his pride and ambition.

Another point to keep in mind about story plays is that each scene should follow the same structure that the play as a whole does, and generally so should each act. That means there is an inciting incident or a change of some sort in the direction of the action until this particular complication is solved. There are two ways of defining scenes, although they are similar in that both begin and end with a change in the complications or the crises. A scene can be thought of as a motivational unit, in which the protagonist has a goal he or she has to achieve. To go back to the analogy of the burning building, each new scene would occur when the circumstances changed. There is the matter of opening the door, escaping through the hallway and so forth. They all contribute to the major goal of getting away from the building, but each is slightly different. Another way of looking at a scene is that it begins with the entrance of a secondary or major character and ends with an exit by a major or secondary character. This is called a French scene, and it stands to reason that the direction would somewhat change when an important character enters or exits. But there also are times that the motivation can change without an entrance or exit. For instance, a character may suddenly be reminded of something which brings about a change in the conflict. Or one character may say something that triggers a new emotional response in another.

One of the most important things to remember about all this is that a crisis should continue to build, and that changes in direction and emotional pitch are needed so a particular emotion or level of intensity will not be maintained for a long period. Also the climax, when it comes, should be inevitable yet somewhat unexpected.

Generally, it's good to keep in mind that there usually are less complications in a tragedy than in a comedy, and they are more serious in nature. Comedy often contains a great many reversals and complications, though many are superficial. The unexpected provides the humor, and the audience doesn't identify so strongly with the characters.

As is apparent, this chapter has dealt with the structure of a full-length play. The one-act has not been discussed because it seems that rather than being easier to write, it is harder. First, it often is difficult to find a worthwhile theme that can can be treated in half an hour or forty-five minutes. Second, the structure of such a play has be be so tight that there can be little freedom for the playwright to develop character, dialogue or plot.

OTHER TYPES OF STRUCTURES

There are several other types of play structure evident in contemporary theatre. One is the play that is unified around a particular theme. It may have a multiplicity of scenes all dealing with the same basic issues but unrelated to each other in continuity or in characterization. Obviously, there would not be as much empathy on the part of the audience, but on the other hand, the message conceivably could be brought out in a more straightforward manner than would be the case with a story play. The drama that relies on theme for unity could often be episodic with various situations dealing with the same subject but taking place with different characters in different locations. Or it might be like some of the Absurdist plays that deal with a single set of characters. An example is Beckett's <u>Waiting for Godot</u>. Many such plays show no real progression of events but do bring home the message of lack of communication or nonawareness.

A play may be presented just to portray a facet of life or a way of life. One such play that has strong characterizations but no real cause-to-effect plot structure is <u>The Effects of Gamma Rays on Man in the Moon Marigolds</u>. It deals largely with the relationships among a mother and two daughters. Such plays often have the purpose of presenting a vignette or an impression, or maybe the writer just wants to express a viewpoint of life and have the audience compare it with theirs.

Another type of play that has been seen in recent years is the one in which current issues are explored. There is nothing new in this concept, except perhaps in the manner of depiction. These plays often are much more subjective than other types, particularly in reference to the issues the playwright is discussing. Because of this, there is a risk of audience alienation. An example would be guerrilla theatre and plays popular in the late sixties and early seventies protesting U.S. involvement in Viet Nam.

Sometimes plays without a plot show incidents following each other in chronological order but not necessarily growing out of the preceding material. In this way they differ from the story play.

There is nothing wrong with following new trends in writing a play or even in experimenting with something entirely your own. If there were, the theatre would be a very static institution, if it existed at all. The new forms are beneficial. They make people realize what the theatre is capable of accomplishing, whether the audience agrees with the techniques or not. Generally, most of the new forms die out after a few years. But their influence is still felt. Overall, change in the theatre is a slow process and there are no overnight revolutions. At best the new trends become incorporated into the older forms which as a result undergo a slight change. Thus theatre progresses.

Many plays are popular during any period only because of their impact on the contemporary circumstances. If some of them were delayed for only a season in being produced, they would mean little. For instance, the issues of draft evasion, dress codes and facing up to responsibility explored in <u>Hair</u>, an extremely popular musical of the Sixties, don't mean nearly so much now as they did then. The play is very much dated.

For a play to be lasting the playwright needs to dig a little more deeply to come up with a theme that is both immediate and universal. If the play is worth writing, it's worth a deeper probing and analysis. Examination of motives on the part of the playwright is the first step in such an analysis.

SUMMARY

It's best to learn the rules of the story play when beginning to write because this form is the most traditional and draws the largest audiences. This type of play has a cause-to-effect relationship in that something happens which presents an obstacle or major problem to the central character. This character than acts to bring about a resolution of the problem. The plot is composed of the inciting incident where the problem is introduced; the rising action, which constitutes a series of complications in the protagonist's attempts at reaching the goal; the turning point, where the action can go no further without the problem being resolved; the climax, where the problem is resolved, and the falling action, which answers anything left unanswered in the rest of the play.

The story play consists largely of conflict or struggle, all of which has to be motivated. Such motivation is dramatic action, which has to have a direct bearing on the struggle and the outcome. Everything in the play should contribute to the dramatic action and the progression of the plot. Dramatic action is composed of a series of small crises and climaxes, each of which serves to introduce the one following. Each helps to reveal the character by showing how the protagonist reacts, and the protagonist should always be the point of focus. All action relates to this person, even when he or she is not physically present.

Interest is maintained through selectivity, contrast and unity. Contrast is needed to provide variety and can occur in the differences among the characters and in the varied series of events in the play. Unity is provided through the action's relating to the cause-to-effect relationship of the plot. There also can be unity of idea and theme.

Each act should contain neither too little nor too much, or the interest of the audience will be lost. Each act must end on a high point to maintain audience interest. If the climax comes late in the play, there will be little time for the unraveling. If it is too early, there is little reason for the rest of the play. It's best to use divisions within an act sparingly, or the play may lag or appear episodic.

The outcome of the play should be determined by the central character, whose actions bring about the resolutions.

Besides the story play, there are other types with which the playwright can experiment. Included are those unified around a particular theme, those which are written just to present a view of life and those dealing with a particular current issue.

EXERCISES

1. Read a play and determine where the inciting incident, the turning point and the climax occur.

2. Take one of the characters you previously developed and determine a major problem with which he or she could be confronted and which could provide the basis for a story play.

3. Read another play and determine its probable effectiveness in holding the audience's attention. How has the writer built the rising action and suspense? Determine the series of crises introduced into one of the acts.

4. Using the central character you have developed, write a scene in which the person is not in direct conflict with the antagonist but in which the conflict is inherent.

80

5. Read a play and determine what actions best reveal the traits of the central character.

6. Read another play and determine its sources of unity. Analyze their effectiveness. What provides the contrast? Determine if the progression of events is logical and well-founded.

7. Read another full-length play and determine how effective the playwright was in ending each act. Was the placement of the climax appropriate? Is the denouement handled effectively? Why or why not?

8. Read a play that does not follow a cause-to-effect relationship. What is its purpose? How is it unified? Could it be effectively presented?

CHAPTER VII

PLANNING AND REVISING YOUR SCRIPT

There are writers who state that they put on paper whatever comes to them without having any kind of guide or outline. These people are rare. Usually, it takes time for an idea to germinate and to grow. Most writers have some sort of an idea about the progression of events, the theme or even the type of resolution. Some prefer to work out an intricate scenario before ever starting to write. Others have just a minimal outline, while some rely only on notes. There are even those who prefer to think through the entire play before putting down a single word. It doesn't matter what approach you take. It matters only which one works for you.

One advantage of detailed planning is that the writing may get started and progress faster than if one does little planning. Another benefit is that a detailed plan may show the strengths and weaknesses of the proposed play. You can see if the relationships are logical and if the characters have strong enough differences to provide conflict. You can judge if the intended structure is interesting. The outline or scenario also can tell you if each act ending is strong enough to maintain interest for the remainder of the play, if the plot progression is clearly worked out and if the theme is well established. You should be able to tell with a detailed plan whether the play has proper balance and whether there is enough emphasis on the important elements of the plot or characterization.

A disadvantage is that the play may become too rigid, and you may have trouble finding enough for the characters to do or say.

The scenario is a device to aid in the development of a play and should be regarded as such. Exploit it as much as you can but don't use it as a crutch.

DETAILS OF THE PLANNING

In planning the script beforehand, you can analyze the characters and their relationship to each other. The type of setting can also be planned. If you know your characters, you probably will know the type of places where they will be found. Planning the setting doesn't necessarily mean working it out in detail. Some writers find it enough, for instance, to indicate that the action takes place in a lower-middle class apartment in Manhattan. Others find it better to have the entire setting in mind because then they can visualize the characters and the actions more clearly.

Often the progression of the play will suggest some details of setting. If the characters become angry with each other and one walks out of the room where the action is taking place, an exit is necessary. Maybe he or she wants to go to a bedroom, or at least the doorway to a bedroom may be suggested as part of the detail.

When a person is writing, he or she often doesn't want to be interrupted or have to slow down the dialogue to write stage directions or details of setting. The important thing is to keep the writing fluid. The setting can be changed or worked out in detail later. It's important in creating atmosphere, but it's not nearly as important in the first writing as are the action, the dialogue and the characters.

The next thing that can be included as part of the scenario is an indication of what the theme of the play will be.

EXPOSITION

Expository material necessary to the understanding of the play also can be planned. Generally, most of it can be worked out along with the character analysis. But since exposition is an important part of the play, you may want to write it all down before beginning the script. That way you can be sure everything needed is included where it's logical and doesn't intrude on the progression of the plot. Much of it, therefore, may have to be written into the script in a more analytical manner after the first draft is completed.

Remember that exposition is anything the audience needs to know about prior events, given circumstances, personality traits, the current situation or relationship among characters to have an understanding of the action.

There are two types of exposition. The first involves only background material and takes more detailed planning. The other type is related to the changing situations. For example, certain feelings a character has may not be so important at the beginning of the play as they are when the character comes up against an obstacle. But to understand his or her reaction to a situation, the audience must know the character's feelings at the present time, and what causes a particular reaction. This second type, the progressive exposition, involves the revelation of character. This constant revelation maintains audience interest and causes the spectators to empathize with the character. If the audience knows beforehand exactly how a character feels or what the person is likely to do in any given situation, there probably would not be much to hold their attention throughout the play. Of course, such exposition needs to be consistent with the image the character projects. What he or she does in certain situations may come as a shock but nevertheless must be logical within the framework of the play.

Exposition is considered in terms of background information pertaining to character. But it may also deal with the opening situation of the play. What are the general economic conditions not only of the characters but also of the world in which they exist? Where does the action take place? Is there anything the audience needs to know about that location? Is it a desolate farmhouse, easily accessible to pranksters or thieves? Is it a slum area where stepping outside can mean being assaulted and beaten? What is the condition of the city or the country where the action takes place? What are the prevailing attitudes of the population? What are the feelings of the time? How do the central and secondary characters' feelings mesh with what their country or the world in general believes? Such questions need to be considered to determine if they are an important aspect of the play.

If the play takes place in another time or location, what are the prevailing conditions? Are the natural laws the same as would be expected in our own world or in our own time? Setting forth exposition of this sort is establishing a frame of reference.

Often it is difficult to find a way of including the necessary exposition in the opening scenes of a play. There are many techniques for doing so, from the Stage Manager in <u>Our Town</u> filling in the audience about Grovers Corners and the people who live there, to a person being interviewed.

Another method is the flashback. In <u>Death of a</u>

85

Salesman we discover quite a bit about Willy's attitudes and feelings because of the first flashback scene with Biff and Happy. We find out why Biff hasn't allowed himself to become successful when we witness the scene at the hotel where Willy has a woman in his room. If the technique can be presented as believable, it can be used. But it must be logical and not call attention to itself.

It often is possible to work the exposition into the scene bit by bit and make it appear realistic. It doesn't all have to be presented at once, as often was the case when prologues were in vogue. An audience doesn't want to sit still in the modern theatre to hear a recitation of facts, nor will they even be able to absorb these facts if they are given one after another. You must judge if the expository material really is necessary. If not, don't include it.

Generally, the exposition should concern the main characters and the overall context of the play. It isn't as necessary to present material about the secondary characters as they would take the focus off the central character.

If you rank the expository material in the order by which it needs to be known, it can be woven into the script more skillfully and more gradually. What the audience needs to know, for instance, at the beginning of the second act may not have been necessary for them to know at the beginning of the play. The audience shouldn't be aware that they are being given expository material, but only that the play is a complete unit within itself and that it accomplishes its aim.

THE STORY LINE

The next thing that can be planned is the action or progression of the play. This means taking into account the inciting incident, the rising action, the turning point and climax and the denouement.

There are two methods of planning scenes. It is a matter of preference in deciding which to use. The first is an outline:

Act I

Scene 1

Scene 2

86

Act II

    Scene 1

    Scene 2

    Scene 3

Act III

For each division you include the characters, the location, the time and a description of the action. The emotional content might also be included. For example:

I. Act I

A. Scene 1

1. Characters--Jim and Helen Peters.

2. Location---The Peters' living room.

3. Time---Friday at 6 p.m.

4. Progression of the action.

    a. Helen has just learned of her brother's death.

    b. Jim comes home from work.

    c. Jim and Helen consider the advisability of going to the town where her brother lived to investigate his death.

    d. Helen becomes hysterical when Jim objects to going.

Just a bare outline is followed to allow freedom in the development. The rest can be filled in during the writing of the first draft. But you should not feel bound to follow the outline rigidly. If the characters want to go in another direction, let them.

You can always pull them back later or rewrite.

The second method some playwrights use is to write a skeletal version of the script, using actual dialogue.

One final thing the planning should include is a title for the play. It not only gives you a psychological boost, but a good title should say something definite about the events of the play or about its theme, and so can help give the script direction. You can begin with any scene or act you choose when writing the rough draft. Some writers prefer to start with the first scene of Act I and write the play in order. Others prefer to start with some other scene. All that matters is getting started at whatever point you think is best.

REVISING THE PLAY

Although it may seem that much of the work of writing a play is finished with the completion of the preliminary outline and the subsequent writing of the rough draft, the work is just beginning. It would be rare to complete the rough draft and have a finished product.

It's not at all unlikely that you may have to do four or five drafts before you are satisfied. There may be a need to rearrange scenes that have been written. A play doesn't always have to follow a chronological order, as can be seen in the use of flashbacks. In addition to any rearranging, you may discover that new scenes or dialogue are needed for clarity. Perhaps a scene just does not come across as you intended when you first wrote the material.

Although the characters should be on their own the first time through a scene, during subsequent drafts you need to assist them. How many times have you been in a situation where you couldn't think of what you wanted to say or when you were too angry to think of an appropriate reply? You later thought back and determined what you might have said. The same thing can happen with characters in a play. But they do have a second chance, and you can give it to them through the rewriting.

Now also is a good idea to read the play aloud or have it read aloud as often as possible to be able to better judge how the dialogue sounds. If possible, you may want to have people who have acting experience read your material. They often have a good feel for what is right and also may be able to point out any awkward phrasing or other difficulties.

You should not hesitate to throw out a scene that doesn't quite say what was intended or that isn't important. This is hard to do since writers are protective of their work. In a scene in my own play discussed in Chapter III, the daughter, Susie, met after school with a friend, at which time she let out all the frustrations she felt in living with Rita and Howie. There was nothing wrong with the scene, and it could have been effective except for two things. First, it took place in a restaurant while the rest of the play occurred in an apartment. For a single scene of ten to twelve minutes, there would have been a need for a different setting and a new character who was not really necessary. It could be just as effective for Susie and her brother, Billy, to have a scene together while Howie and Rita were gone. In this new scene which I wrote they both discuss their frustrations and give each other moral support. Thus, more of Billy's character, as well as Susie's, could be revealed, providing the second reason for cutting the original scene.

Much of the work of revising is in tightening scenes and dialogue. Sometimes as much as half of what you have written can be eliminated because it will be repetitive or lack direction.

During the revision you can plan the setting exactly the way you want it. Now is the time to consider it practically. Generally, it's better to have as few changes of scenery as possible due to the expense of building sets and the necessity of making the audience wait while the scenery is shifted. If you are planning to use mostly lighting for effect and suggestive scenery rather than that which portrays place, this matter becomes less important. But there is still the risk of confusing the audience as to where the characters are in any given situation.

There are several functions of setting. One is to provide the proper atmosphere. If the location is a dwelling, the audience should be able to recognize the economic situation of the characters. Another function of the set is to reflect the interests of the characters and tell something about their personalities. Much of the detail will be up to the designer, but you should certainly keep in mind what is needed for exposition and to provide a proper environment or background for the action. If you don't plan the setting well, even though it may later be changed by the designer and the director, it could mean you are rather vague about the play's direction. The primary concern is clarity.

You don't have to be an expert designer, but you should know what works and what doesn't. If you at least are acquainted with design and construction, you will be better able to write a play that can be practicably executed. For instance, it would be impractical to have the action take place in three large, completely furnished apartments. Backstage storage alone would create problems.

The final consideration in revising the script is the matter of stage directions. Generally, the fewer the better. It's pointless to include long passages about how the setting would be used and how the actors should move and react. Directors want to have their own say about what is to be done.

SUMMARY

Some writers prefer to work out in detail the progression of the plot. Others make notes, while still others begin to write without much planning at all. It doesn't matter which method is used. It matter only that the playwright discover which method works best for him or her. A playwright should know the characters and their relationship before beginning the writing.

Some writers also prefer to plan out the details of setting before beginning to write; others prefer to begin just with a vague impression and let the action of the play determine specific elements of the set. Either method is workable. Often, too, a playwright will want to wait until the first draft is finished before including stage directions, as stopping to include them may slow down the writing.

Too much planning may make the script appear rigid and artificial, whereas not enough may make the plot lack direction. Often it works well to list any expository material necessary to the understanding of the play before beginning to write. You can rank it in order of importance, and by referring to the list can ometimes determine during the writing where the material should be included.

There are two types of exposition. The first gives any background material necessary to an understanding of the play. The other deals with revelations in character or events as the play progresses. The second type is what generally provides the interest and suspense of the plot.

You should attempt to work out a way to include the expository material without making the audience aware that they are receiving it. In planning the story line you can either outline the action or use a scenario.

After the rough draft is finished, there is still much work to be done. Revision includes selecting and heightening scenes to make the play more unified, planning the setting in a more detailed manner and writing stage directions.

EXERCISES

1. Using the central character and the situations you previously wrote, develop a plan for a full-length play.

2. Make a list of the background exposition that is necessary. Rank it in order of importance.

3. Determine the type of setting you want to use.

4. Write a scene in which you include all necessary stage directions.

5. Determine any special conditions of time, place, or general attitude that will affect the progression of your play.

6. Write a scene in which you include background exposition.

7. On the basis of what you have already planned, make a list of the properties you will need. Include those essential to the plot as well as those for mood and atmosphere.

8. Take a scene you have written and revise it as completely to your satisfaction as you can.

CHAPTER VIII

GENRE, STYLE AND ENVIRONMENT

It's difficult to categorize many modern plays since there is a strong overlapping and a mixture of various elements. There are plays that basically are comedies but have tragic elements, and tragedies that contain elements of comedy. If we take the oldest definition of tragedy as a form that "shows noble actions of noble men," we have few modern tragedies. There are plays that are serious in theme but do not end in the death of the protagonist. An example is Williams The Glass Menagerie.

GENRE

Genre refers to the way playwrights treat the subject matter about which they are writing. The treatment is related to their outlook which in turn affects the purpose in writing. Purpose is closely related to the treatment of a particular subject or theme. What is depicted should be the truth of the human condition as the playwright sees it. Whether this depiction takes the form of comedy, farce, tragedy or melodrama doesn't matter. The only thing that does matter is the success of the play, whether it's to ridicule and change something or to present a nostalgic view of a bygone era.

To be able to choose the right genre, you need to be acquainted with the different forms drama can take. Overall, there are two methods of treating subject matter, serious and comic. Within these broad categories fall all the various labels of plays.

Closely related to genre are the representational and presentational styles. The former contributes to empathy, the latter to aesthetic distance. An audience can be reached by making them feel what the character is feeling. And a play that leans heavily in this direction is serious in nature. On the other hand, the audience can be approached through the intellect. Comedy is funny because of aesthetic distance. In real life, a man's tripping over a rock and breaking a leg wouldn't be funny. In a comedy it might be. The reason is that we don't closely identify with the leading characters in most comedies. We keep our aesthetic distance. A way of looking at the difference between the two is to think of a raging fire. If we

93

see it on television and know it was set to test
firefighting equipment, it can have a certain beauty.
But if it's burning down our house, we are affected
emotionally. The first instance doesn't affect us
personally, while the second does. This is the
difference between aesthetic distance and empathy.

Most plays are neither pure presentation nor pure
representation but a mixture. That is what on one hand
allows us to identify with the character in a play and
feel the emotion he or she feels, while at the same
time stops us from running onto the stage to help out
when the character is in difficulty.

There is no real separation of the two concepts,
but a balance must be maintained. If we empathize too
much, we lose our objectivity. If we don't identify
enough, the play has no meaning.

Tragedy

The most basic genre for serious treatment of a
theme and so the most representational is tragedy. The
writer tries to have the audience identify completely
with the protagonist who after struggling against
overwhelming odds is defeated.

Aristotle said that tragedy "is an imitation of an
action that is serious, complete, and of a certain
magnitude; in language embellished with each kind of
artistic ornament, the several kinds being found in
separate parts of the play; in the form of action, not
narrative; through pity and fear effecting the proper
purgation of these emotions."

Many theatre theorists believe that all tragedy
must follow this definition, that it has to deal with
highly serious and profound problems. Often it deals
with human nature at its most basic, the struggle of
good and evil. Tragic protagonists either battle a
flaw in themselves or evil in others. The forces are
always more powerful than they are. But through defeat
they remain noble and in this respect are triumphant.

The purpose of tragedy is to make the audience
feel through identification with the tragic hero and
his or her struggles. Because of tragedy's elevated
spirit, the language generally is on a higher plane.
Also to be most effective, according to Aristotle, a
tragedy must be presented in the form of action. Only
if we see what the tragic hero does can we identify

with the person. We can feel compassion and share in the suffering. We grieve at the tragic hero's defeat, which is what Aristotle meant by pity. The "fear" is the anxiety aroused by viewing the play, and it then should carry over in our concern for others.

The "purgation of emotions" means a release of emotional tension, a catharsis, that leaves us at peace. We have identified with a noble character, a human being like ourselves. Therefore we must to a degree possess the character's nobility and positive traits. When the protagonist pursues a goal to the end, we feel the same strength and persistence in ourselves. If the character is good, we too have the capacity for goodness, reaffirmed by the protagonist's noble battle. We suffer with the character but can in a way feel superior. The protagonist has suffered a defeat whereas we are safe and will not have to be defeated. Above all, tragedy reaffirms our faith in ourselves as part of the human race. Even when tragic characters die, their heroism lives. Not their deaths but what the playwright says about life is important.

Even though we suffer with the tragic hero, we find aesthetic beauty in the drama with its grandeur of character, theme and action.

The workings of the protagonist's mind are the most important aspect of a tragedy. It's how the character reacts that gives us tragedy, so the writer has to be a skilled analyst of human behavior. The playwright makes us feel we are experienceing the struggle and death of someone close to us. Although they are good, tragic heroes are imperfect. Because of their weaknesses, we can relate better to them.

The playwright tries to show life as it is, except perhaps for the grandeur and loftiness. Tragic heroes face the consequences of their actions and realize that they will be defeated. But along the way they experience new insights into themselves as the audience experiences insights into themselves.

Comedy

The opposite of tragedy is comedy which has the purpose of making us laugh. Most often we are asked to laugh at ourselves and our institutions so that we'll take ourselves less seriously.

Whereas tragedy is a fairly narrow form, comedy

has the greatest variety of any genre of drama. It can be slapstick or gentle. It most often shows a deviation from the norm of everyday life, even though it often is concerned with the mundane and the pettiness of day-to-day living.

Comedy has a variety of purposes in making us laugh, and they differ from play to play. At times the writer may want to have us take ourselves less seriously or to free us from tension, even if just for a couple of hours. Many times the writer of comedy reminds us of our own frailties but is telling us they aren't so serious as we sometimes think. Another purpose of comedy may be to correct social injustice. The idea is that if we can laugh at social and character flaws, maybe then we will be more inclined to correct them. Comedy also keeps us from gaining too high an opinion of ourselves. In this way it's corrective.

The humor in a comedy can come from the treatment of character or situations. It forces us to view objectively any deviation. Any subject matter can be used if it can be treated in a humorous light. It's only if the deviation from the norm becomes too painful or too severe that the comedy suffers and ceases to be funny. It would be cruel and unfunny to treat physical deformities or handicaps as sources of comedy. More often it is the things over which we have control or our views of uncontrollable forces that comprise the subject matter.

Such things as eccentricities of character can be humorous, as is Moliere's treatment of Harpagon's greed in The Miser. Other character traits that might be the basis of comedy are hypocrisy, laziness or overwhelming ambition. Humorous treatment of situations also can be the basis of humor. For instance, comic protagonists may become involved in situations with which they are unable to cope or which are outside their knowledge and experience. An example might be a plumber posing as a brain surgeon. In effect, comedy ridicules our tendency to be what we are not or to place too much importance on our involvements and our goals.

Unlike tragedy, comedy must end happily. The protagonist has to win. If he or she were to be defeated, the audience would feel guilt or shame for having laughed at the character. So it's important that a comic frame of reference be developed. If the audience isn't given this frame of reference, they may

96

not know how to respond. The spectators should know that what they are seeing isn't to be taken seriously, and they aren't expected to identify either with the character or the situation, unless it's a matter of laughing with instead of at the protagonist.

There are certain devices that can help establish a comic frame of reference. They are **derision, incongruity, exaggeration, repetition, surprise** and **character inconsistency.**

Derision means laughing at people or institutions by poking fun at them. Its object is to deflate egos or cause discomfort. It can be effective but often runs the risk of seeming too bitter. If it is, the audience may then identify with the intended victim.

Incongruity involves opposites or different elements seen together in deviation from the norm. An example is a tall woman with a short man.

Exaggeration means enlargement through overstatement. For example, people are not as greedy as Moliere's character, Harpagon. Exaggeration often encompasses the other comic devices by heightening them.

Repetition includes the verbal or visual gag that is done over and over. An example would be a man's tripping over a stool each time he enters or exits.

Surprise simply is the unexpected. We know every joke will have a punch line which we anticipate. But even though we know it's coming, the punch line is unexpected in what it contains. Surprise includes the pun, the insult or other verbal wit in a play.

Character inconsistency means a personality trait that doesn't seem to fit with the others. An example would be a murderer who helps old women across the street.

Closely related to derision but often considered a sub-genre of comedy is satire, which ridicules for the purpose of reform but is gentler.

Melodrama

Another genre is melodrama, which combines some of the elements of comedy with those of tragedy. It's similar to comedy in that it most often has a happy

97

ending. It's related to tragedy in that it treats a serious subject and the audience identifies or empathizes with the characters. But unlike tragic characters those in melodrama are one-dimensional.

Melodrama often relies on creating feelings of terror, and coincidence or fate plays a large part in the outcome. Good always triumphs. The form includes sentimentality. It is often episodic in that the most exciting events and situations are included in the script. There also is comic relief in the form of the minor characters.

Farce

A fourth genre is farce, similar to melodrama in that fate often plays a part in the outcome. But it's more closely related to comedy, and its main purpose is entertainment. It uses stock characters with no depth, and the plots, highly contrived, rely on physical actions and devious twists. There is never any important theme, and the progression shows only how the major characters manage to release themselves from entanglements.

Although farce often deals with illicit sexual relationships and infidelity, its outlook is amoral. The aim is only to provide laughter for the audience, and much of the fun is in the visual gags and absurdities of speech. The plot relies on misunderstandings, and many of the comic devices are used, including repetition, incongruity and derision. There often are physical violence, misunderstandings, mistaken identity and deception. The characters are victims of their vices and appear ridiculous when caught.

There are various other genres. One is **tragicomedy**, which mingles elements of the comic and serious. Often the terms is applied to Absurdist plays. The term is paradoxical in that a protagonist who is truly noble cannot appear comic, nor can a comic protagonist possess the scope of a tragic hero. Nevertheless, some playwrights do mingle comic and tragic elements, but it takes a skillful writer to do this without confusing the audience. Often a situation appears comic, but later the audience realizes it's serious. Tragicomedy generally tries to show how life intermingles the comic and the tragic.

There are various other kinds of plays that do not

seem to fit any particular genre. Some, such as A Raisin in the Sun, possess more scope than melodrama, yet do not end in the protagonist's defeat. Sometimes three-dimensional characters are presented in plays that are neither tragic nor comic, as is the case with The Glass Menagerie, with deals with people who are trapped by circumstances and their own limitations. During the course of the play, the characters are not defeated. Instead the defeat has started long before the play opens.

It is a good idea to be acquainted with all the different genres to know what can be made to work.

DEFINITION OF STYLE

Style refers to the manner in which the play both is written and designed and results largely from the way the playwrights view the subjects with which they are dealing. In other words, the play's structure and form both relate to and merge with the style of the production. The representational style, as you learned, attempts to imitate reality, and the audience empathizes more fully with the characters and the situation. A danger with this style is that if there is too much detail in trying to depict life, either in the setting or in the play itself, there's no focal point for the audience, and the production lacks any real meaning. The presentational style, on the other hand, is audience-centered. It proclaims that theatre comes from life but definitely is not life. It can lack any real communication with the audience if carried to extremes because it becomes too far separated from life.

Style is just a basic approach to a play or a production, and none is pure. Every play is a mixing of two or more styles, but the style of the production and that of the script have to match. There are some plays that demand a particular approach, while others could be done in a variety of basic styles in production.

The most representational style is **naturalism,** which attempts to present life as it actually is. In pure naturalism an attempt is made to include everything found in life. In writing this means including all the details of conversation and physical movement. In setting it means including everything that would be found in an actual dwelling or location. Even those things that are never used by the actors have to be real. All windows have to open, all fireplaces work and all costumes match those in everyday life. Of course, there can be no such thing as pure naturalism because everything in life can't be exactly duplicated for the theatre, nor can life exist onstage as it does outside the theatre.

Realism is close to naturalism in that an attempt is made to convince the audience that what they are viewing is life, although realism is selective in that it doesn't include every detail. Anything needed to convey a mood or atmosphere or to portray character can be included whether it's actually used in the play or not. Realistic dialogue is made to sound like that of life except that it is more selective. It has less extraneous detail and more direction. Another difference between naturalism and realism is that although details may be included to convey mood or character, they needn't be the actual object nor do they need to be practical. Sometimes, there is a further style differentiated from realism and called **selective realism**. This doesn't mean much in itself but is only a matter of degree. Only those parts of the setting or those properties that are ever used are seen. With selective realism the objects seen onstage should appear to be just like those in life, although they can actually be substitutes.

A style that is more audience-centered but still has some elements of the representational is **expressionism**. The central character is seen as his or her inner self. The setting relies on the script to provide the answers as to how the protagonist views life. This viewpoint then is expressed in the setting. This requires a close meshing of styles of writing and design. In other words, the audience is made to see reality as the protagonist sees it.

Impressionism deals with the design, exclusive of any actual conditions demanded by the script. That is, the designer and the director figure out what they want to stress most in the setting, and this element is applied externally to the production. Impressionism usually is very selective in what is shown. It is, in effect, the director and/or designer giving an impression of the play.

In **symbolism**, the playwright presents life allegorically in conveying any message or sense ·of truth. The set likewise is more presentational than that of many other styles and doesn't attempt to present a realistic view of life. Often, undefined forms are used only to give a general impression that will convey the playwright's message.

Theatricalism and **formalism** sometimes are considered as styles, but they really are only treatments of other styles. With theatricalism, the designer breaks down any suggestion of a fourth wall and allows the audience members to use their imagination in the matter of setting. The viewer is constantly reminded of being in a theatre in that there often is no attempt to disguise lighting instruments or backstage areas. Only those elements of setting that are needed are used. Formalism, which overlaps theatricalism or impressionism, uses only what is necessary to the actor and then only because it's there. For instance, rather than flats, drapes may be used for concealment or for exits and entrances.

THE SETTING

There are several functions of setting beyond acting as a channel for the playwright's message. One is to provide information essential to the understanding of the play. Setting also indicates the environment, sets the mood and provides a focal point for the audience and a framework for the action.

When first viewed, it prepares the audience for the production. The colors and shapes help convey the style and the genre. Austere lines probably would suggest a tragedy or serious play, while curved lines and splashes of color most likely would suggest a comedy. The audience also can tell if the play is going to be realistic or nonrealistic. The spectator should be able to recognize the environment of the play if it's important to the action. It may locate time and place through the furnishings and may tell us about the tastes, interests and financial condition of the characters. A setting provides a visual image that conveys the play's message and so must be correct aesthetically for each production.

The scenery that is used most often is a **box set** or **flats** fastened together to look like the interior walls of a room or several rooms. The flats are made of one-by-three boards, covered with canvas and painted. They also can be constructed with doors, windows and fireplaces built in. Such scenery often looks as much as possible like an actual location and provides an environment in which the actors perform.

101

The setting surrounds them.

Scenery also comprises various hanging units, including **backdrops**. These are made of theatrical canvas, painted and hung with weights at the bottom, then suspended from a batten and usually stretching across the stage. This type of scenery often provides a background for the action, rather than an environment.

Built units consist of platforms, steps, rocks, columns or different levels to represent hills or rises in the ground. One type is the wagon on which can be placed flats to indicate a room or dwelling. The wagon is built on rollers and is used for shifting scenery silently and effectively. Set units are two-dimensional pieces used to suggest walls, fences or rows of shrubbery. They generally are made of plywood. They are cut out and painted and stand independently.

These are just the basic units, but you should be able to see the kind of thing that might be used for the play you write. Before attempting to complete a play for production, you should learn as much as you can about scenery to understand how it can be used.

THEATRE STRUCTURES

There are three major types of theatre structures in use today, although the styles overlap, and plays are presented in a great variety of locations from large rooms to city parks.

The Proscenium Theatre

The theatre structure that outnumbers all others is the proscenium theatre, often called a picture frame theatre because the stage has an arch that frames the acting area. The audience sits facing the stage and usually is expected to believe that they are viewing the action through an imaginary fourth wall.

There is a psychological as well as a physical separation of the audience and actor, and the setting can be more realistic than it can be in an arena or thrust stage theatre.

When proscenium theatres were first constructed, stages were raked upward to the rear wall. That is why **upstage** means the area furthest from the audience, while that closest to the audience is **downstage**. **Stage Right** is the area to the actors' right as they face the audience. **Up Center** then would be the middle area toward the back and **Down Center** would be the center of the stage closest to the audience. From this it is easy to figure out the other areas such as **Down Right** or **Left Center**. Usually in a script the names are abbreviated, such as **DL** (**Down Left**) or **UR** (**Up Right**). It's important to know these areas since most plays are written for a proscenium stage.

There are several advantages to a proscenium stage. First, the scenery can be more realistic, and the curtain can be closed for scenery shifts. Actors can wait just offstage for their cues, and scenery and props can be stored close to the acting area but away from the audience's view.

Those who use a proscenium stage need to be concerned with presenting a pleasing picture in the composition of the setting and in the placement of the actors.

A disadvantage is that there cannot be the closeness between audience and actor that is desirable for some plays, particularly those done in a presentational style.

The Arena Theatre

In arena theatre, or theatre-in-the-round as it's often called, the audience surrounds the action. The acting area in this type of theatre, with historical precedent in the theatres of ancient Greece, usually is square or oval rather than round. Whereas in proscenium theatre the stage usually is raised above the audience, in arena theatre the acting area is lower. The seats are raked downward from the outer walls of the theatre toward the stage.

Since the audience surrounds the action, there can be no definite stage areas as there are in proscenium theatre, nor can realistic sets be used. But properties have to be more realistic for representational plays because the audience usually is closer to the action and can easily detect any poor substitutes. Makeup also is more subtle.

An advantage is the closeness between spectator and actor, and there can be more intimacy. A playwright who wants to communicate directly to the

103

audience can do it more easily in an arena theatre.

The major disadvantage is that it is difficult to conceal anything. Actors cannot wait offstage but may have to make longer entrances and exits, and properties not in use either have to be stored in sight of the audience or have to be carried through the aisleways to the acting area.

The Thrust Stage

Another type of theatre is one that contains a thrust stage with a playing area similar to that of the arena theatre, except that one side opens into a stagehouse or back wall. The audience sits around the three remaining sides. Most often this kind of stage is lower than the audience, though occasionally it's higher.

Since there is a back wall, more scenery can be used than in arena theatre but not as much as on a proscenium stage. There can be no box sets used, but at least there can be a background for the actors. As in arena theatre, the audience is closer to the actor, and there is no physical separation such as there is in the proscenium arch.

There are various other stages, but they are simply modifications of these three. Some have a proscenium stage with a large apron or forestage that extends out toward the audience in front of the proscenium arch. Some platform stages are built without framing devices, and some theatres have ramps extending into the audience or side stages, small acting areas outside the proscenium arch and on either side of the main stage.

A great deal of difference exists among theatres of a particular type. Some proscenium theatres seat few spectators while other seat hundreds. Of course, intimate plays would be less effective in a large theatre, and elaborate productions would suffer in a theatre that seats less than a hundred.

SUMMARY

The playwright should be acquainted with the forms of drama, the styles of production and the types of theatre structures where original plays might be produced.

Basically, there are two forms of drama, the serious and the comic. The genre is determined in large part by how playwrights view the world and consequently how they treat the subject matter about which they are writing. The most serious genre is tragedy, which attempts to have the audience identify fully with the protagonist, who finally is defeated. Comedy has a wider scope and attempts to show life more objectively and asks more detachment on the part of the viewer. Comedy deals with deviations from the norm and relies for its humor on situations and character. In a comedy the protagonist is triumphant. A third genre is melodrama, which mixes comic and tragic elements. It relies strongly on coincidence and depicts a strong separation of good and evil. It always ends happily. Another genre is farce, which is amoral in outlook and exists purely for entertainment. There are various other genres that mingle elements from the more familiar ones.

There are two basic styles of production and writing, the representational and the presentational. The former tries to imitate and portray life, while the latter only suggests life. Other styles that have grown out of these two are naturalism, which attempts to show life as it actually is; realism, which depicts life but is selective in the elements used; expressionism, which attempts to show the feelings or inner workings of the protagonist's mind; impressionism, in which the designer and director are selective in giving their impressions of the play, and symbolism, which presents life allegorically. Theatricalism and formalism are approaches to other styles.

Setting provides a channel for the playwright's message and presents information essential to the understanding of the play. It also tells the audience the type of play to expect.

Basic types of scenery are flats, hanging units, built units and set units or two-dimensional pieces that stand independently.

The main types of theatres are the proscenium, the arena and the thrust stage. The proscenium stage physically separates the audience and the actor and frames the action of the play. Settings for this style of theatre can be more realistic than those in an arena theatre. An arena stage is one in which the audience surrounds the playing area. The settings must be more suggestive than realistic, and there are problems of concealment. But there can be more intimacy between actor and audience. The third type is the thrust-stage theatre. The audience sits on three sides while the fourth opens into a stagehouse or back wall.

EXERCISES

1. Read a comedy, a farce and a satire. Evaluate the elements from each that determine the genre.

2. Read a contemporary melodrama. Compare it with a nineteenth-century melodrama.

3. Read a Greek tragedy and compare its effectiveness with that of a recent tragedy.

4. Take the play you are planning and determine what form it will take. Try to determine if and why this form is appropriate to your subject matter and treatment.

5. Read another comedy. What comic devices did the author use? Try to determine what makes the play effective.

6. Find a play that is largely presentational and one that is largely representational. Compare the two as to technique and effectiveness. What elements of representation and presentation does each possess?

7. What is the predominant style of the play you are writing? Why did you choose this style? Could another be used effectively?

8. Read a symbolic play or naturalistic play. Analyze the elements of the style and the effectiveness of the techniques the playwright chose to use that coincide with that style.

9. Analyze in detail the type of setting that could be used for the play you are writing. Determine its practicability in terms of construction and shifting. Could another type of setting be used?

10. If your play is intended primarily for a proscenium theatre, could it be adapted to arena staging? If for arena, determine its adaptability to proscenium staging.

CHAPTER IX

MARKETING YOUR PLAY

After your play is finished, the important thing is to have it produced. If you've defined the type of audience for whom you are writing, you should have little trouble choosing a specific market.

There are certain things you should do before rushing to the post office with the script. The first is to be certain that your play is as polished as you can make it. This means a lot of revision. Of course, if you haven't already, you should seek the critical opinion of others, those who will be honest with you. Many beginning writers are afraid to allow others to read their work because they don't want to be told the play is lacking in some respect. But it's better to be told any weaknesses the play has before you send it out.

Since a play is intended to be heard and seen and not just read silently, you will want to know how it sounds. It also helps to have someone look over the script for such things as punctuation and spelling. No matter how well you spell or how much you know about grammar, it would be very unlikely not to make a few mistakes in the technical aspects of writing.

It's a good idea to have your play produced in a theatre with which you are affiliated to help you better judge its effectiveness. There are some markets that want only previously produced plays submitted to them. If you write a short story or an article and it's published, it's possible that you will lose many of the rights to it, and selling it again can be rather difficult. Such is not the case with a play. Generally, a producer will take only "run-of-the-play" rights. You should beware of selling a script to a market that wants to buy all the rights since you could lose a great deal of money that way.

If you have the play done by a group with which you are affiliated, the production can be viewed as a tryout period. During the rehearsal time and after the closing, you probably will find that you have some rewriting to do. Even after you sell a play to a professional market, you often are required to attend the rehearsals for the purpose of interpretation and rewriting.

After you have done everything possible in receiving critical opinion of the script, have heard the play read aloud and perhaps have seen it presented, the next thing you will want to do is to prepare a finished copy of your manuscript. The play should look readable and professional. Many original works are never considered seriously because they do not follow an acceptable format. The producers often think, and rightly so, that if the playwright didn't know enough or care enough to type the manuscript correctly, the play cannot be very good. After the final typing, the playwright should take great care with the proofreading, no matter how tedious it is. If the manuscript is carelessly typed and appears messy or is full of errors, the producer will give it little credence.

Another consideration is the paper to be used. It should be a good bond paper of sixteen or twenty pound weight. Don't use erasable paper as it smudges erasily. Standard-sized, white paper only should be used, although if you prefer to send out multiple copies, which is acceptable with a play, you may send out good quality photocopies.

Use a typewriter with either the standard elite or pica type. Stay away from those that use script writing or any exotic style of printing. Your margins should be one inch on the right side, one and a half inches at the left, and an inch and a quarter at the top and bottom.

Page numbers appear in the upper right hand corner of each page of the script. They should include three things: the act number, the scene number, and the page number. For example, the second page of Act I, Scene 1, would be written: I-1-2. The final number begins again with "1" at the beginning of each act. For instance, II-1-1.

Several prefatory pages should be included. The first is the title page, which contains the name of the play in capital letters and centered about a third of the way down the page. The title is underlined. Centered under the title and three spaces down should be the byline with your name in capital letters. The copyright notice appears at the bottom, left-hand side of the page. A sample title page follows.

After the title page is an unnumbered page listing

108

IN REAL LIFE

by JOHN J. JONES

the cast of characters and, if desired, an identification of each. For example:

CAST OF CHARACTERS

JOSEPH SMITH, 39, father of JIM and SUSIE SMITH

HELEN SMITH, 34, wife of JOSEPH

ROBERT BROWN, 65, grandfather of JIM and SUSIE

On the same page as the cast of characters can be the time and place of the action. If there isn't enough room, it can be at the top of the next page. For example:

The action occurs during a weekend in November on the Smith farm in New Hampshire. The time is the present.

The next page, also unnumbered, contains the synopsis of scenes and a description of the setting:

SYNOPSIS OF SCENES

ACT I

The Smith farmhouse. About 2 p.m. Friday.

ACT II

The same. Saturday evening.

ACT III

The same. Saturday evening.

SETTING: The Smith home is a typical farmhouse, constructed in the early twentieth century. The living room contains a few hardbacked chairs, a sofa, and a fireplace. There are a few occasional tables and a painting or two on each of the walls. The floor is covered with a braided rug. One doorway leads to the kitchen; the other leads upstairs. There is a window overlooking the grove, a wooded area with tall shade trees.

Before each act is another unnumbered page, which gives the title of the play, underlined, in caps and centered. Three spaces under the title appears the act designation, also centered and in caps.

The dialogue pages should be set up in the following manner. Characters' names, before their dialogue and in the stage directions, should be in capital letters and approximately four inches from the left-hand margin. All stage directions, except those of a word or two, should also be indented about four inches, in parenthesis, and single spaced. Dialogue begins at the left margin. Everything is single-spaced except that there should be a double space between the final stage direction or dialogue of one character and that of the next character. Directions of only a few words can appear in parenthesis within the lines of dialogue. When a character makes the first appearance, the description should be given in parenthesis in the same manner as a stage direction. Dialogue is never paragraphed, and each scene and act should be ended as follows: END OF ACT II, SCENE 1. Such a notice should be triple-spaced and centered below the last line of the dialogue or stage direction. The words, THE END, should appear at the conclusion of the play.

Another consideration in preparing to send out a manuscript is the matter of copyright. As soon as your play is written, it is protected as "Common Law Literary Property." This form of copyright lasts as long as the work is unpublished or until Statutory Copyright is secured. The latter applies only to unpublished forms such as musical compositions, plays, art works and some other specialized forms.

If you do want to secure a Statutory Copyright, you should register a claim with the Federal Copyright Office. A form can be obtained by writing to: Copyright Office, The Library of Congress, Washington, DC 20540. Request a copy of "Form D," which is the proper one for the copyrighting of plays. After your receive your form, you should fill it out and return it with a copy of your script and the required fee.

Before copyrighting your play, be sure it is revised as completely as possible, and you are ready to send it out. The reason is that the copyright notice lists the year in which the play was registered, and it may appear outdated before you ever send it out. On the other hand, many professional producers won't look at a play that isn't copyrighted.

The next step in marketing your play is to prepare it for mailing. The script should be secured at the

111

                         SARAH
                    (Talking on the telephone.)
I don't know what I'm going to do. I just can't take it.
Twenty-four hours a day and no relief. (Pause.) Well,
maybe sometimes on Friday night when Jim comes down. The
I can go quilting or out to dinner. (Pause.) Well, your
phone bill is going to be awful high, Cathy. I'll call
Saturday night when your Dad comes. He can talk too.

                              (GRANDMA PAULSEN enters from the
                              living room. A tall, thin woman
                              of eighty-six, she is dressed in
                              homemade, flower-print dress, wh
                              fits loosely and comes down a fe
                              inches below her knees. A fadec
                              apron is tied around her waist.
                              She wears heavy brown stockings
                              black oxfords. Slightly stooped
                              she walks very slowly. She wear
                              wire-rimmed glasses and her eyes
                              are always sad. She is mutterir
                              as she enters.)

                         GRANDMA PAULSEN
Well, are you talking to her again? She sure does know h
to waste money.

                         SARAH
                    (She glances toward GRANDMA PAUL
                    before speaking again.)
Well, I guess I better get supper now. We can talk later
Chin up. 'Bye. (Pause.) I love you too.

                         GRANDMA PAULSEN
                    (She sits at the kitchen table.)
Let's have that roast beef tonight that the Fosters gave
you. And maybe some mixed vegetables and canned pears.
don't cook as much as you did at noon. You know I just c
eat much anymore, and Pop doesn't either. (Pause.) And
have to watch your weight, you know. (Pause.) I think v
could use some more coal on that furnace.

                         SARAH
                    (She crosses to the cellar door.
Okay, Mom, but it seems pretty warm in here to me.

                         GRANDMA PAULSEN
Well, I'm cold. Maybe if you'd fix me a cup of coffee,
it would help. You'd better check the furnace, though,
just to be sure.

left side in some sort of cover. It should then be sent in a manila envelope. Be sure to enclose a self-addressed envelope and return postage in the event your script is to be returned. It's best to type mailing labels and paste them to the envelopes, rather than writing on the envelope itself. Again, the reason is that this gives your script a neater and more professional appearance. You should also be aware of the fact that any manuscripts can be mailed at a special fourth class rate, which is considerably less expensive than mailing your submissions at first class rates. First class or priority mail does receive preferential treatment and usually arrives at its destination much more quickly.

One of the most important considerations is choosing an appropriate market. Plays can be submitted to producers, contests, professional theatre companies, educational theatres, community theatres, various summer theatres and publishers. There are many ways of investigating specific markets. One of the best is to find any theatres in your area which would be willing to produce original plays. You may be surprised to learn that they include high schools, colleges, children's theatre groups, community theatres and regional professional theatres.

At a certain point you may find such a listing too limited or else unsuited to your particular play. There are other sources you can investigate. An excellent listing of producers, contests and publishers appears in <u>Writer's Market</u>, published yearly by Writers' Digest Books, 9933 Alliance Road, Cincinnati, Ohio 45242. Available in many book stores, it also may be ordered direct. It includes listings of many of the major New York producers as well as regional theatres in the United States that produce original plays. The magazine, <u>The Writer</u>, sometimes devotes an issue to playwrighting markets and contests.

Another possibility is grants. There are a variety of organizations, including arts councils in many states, that provide grants or aid to playwrights. Some of these also offer an opportunity for production.

It's best to learn as much as you can about the theatres where you may submit your work. Plays often are produced through having the right contacts with producers, directors or actors. Many times, if they know a new playwright, they will be more willing to

113

give him or her a chance. There also are various organizations for playwrights which may give the beginner help and encouragement.

A final word about marketing. Often writers think if they could get an agent to handle their scripts, success would be instantaneous. Such is not the case. First, most agents won't handle the work of a new playwright, and those who do often charge a reading fee of up to several hundred dollars. Since this is the case, it usually is a waste of time and money for the beginner to contact an agent. It's more likely that if you achieve some degree of success, an agent will then be willing to listen or may even contact you. An agent's major function is to handle some of the business details and the matter of contracts. If you do want to contact an agent, you can get a list of those who handle plays by writing to the Society of Authors' Representatives, Inc., 101 Park Ave., New York, New York 10017, or the Authors Guild of America, 6 E. 39th St., New York, New York 10016. You should be careful, however, if you contact those agents who advertise. Although some of them are reputable, many aren't and will promise you success after charging an exorbitant fee for evaluating your script.

In the final analysis, it depends upon you and only you to be successful as a playwright. If you are willing to work hard at both the writing and business ends of getting your script before the public, you have a good portion of the battle won.

SELECTED BIBLIOGRAPHY

Archer, William. *Play-Making: A Manual of Craftsmanship*. New York: Dodd, Mead & Co., 1928.

Baker, George Pierce. *Dramatic Technique*. Boston: Houghton Mifflin Co., 1919.

Busfield, Roger M., Jr. *The Playwright's Art*. New York: Harper & Brothers, 1958.

Egri, Lajos. *The Art of Dramatic Writing*. New York: Simon and Schuster, 1946.

Ervine, St. John. *How to Write a Play*. New York: The Macmillan Co., 1928.

Grenbanier, Bernard. *Playwriting*. New York: Thomas Y. Crowell Co., 1961.

Hatton, Thomas J. *Playwriting for Amateurs*. Downers Grove Illinois: Meriwether Publishing Ltd., 1981

Howard, Louise, and Jeron Criswell. *How Your Play Can Crash Broadway*. New York: Howard and Criswell, 1939.

Hull, Raymond. *How to Write a Play*. Cincinnati: Writer's Digest Books, 1983.

Kerr, Walter. *How Not to Write a Play*. New York: Simon and Schuster, 1955.

Langner, Lawrence. *The Play's the Thing*. New York: G. P. Putnam's Sons, 1960.

Lawson, John Howard. *Theory and Technique of Playwriting*. Copyright, 1936, G. P. Putnam's Sons; rpt. New York: Hill and Wang, 1960.

Matthews, Brander, ed. *Papers on Playmaking*. New York: Hill and Wang, 1957.

Smiley, Sam. *Playwrighting: The Structure of Action*. Englewood Cliffs, New Jersey: Prentice-Hall, Inc., 1971.

Wilder, Thornton. "Preface," *Three Plays by Thornton Wilder*. New York: Harper & Row Publishers, Inc.,

Williams, Tennessee. *Where I Live: Selected Essays*. New York: New Directions, 1978.